IN MY FATHER'S IMAGE

The Father Memories Workbook

RANDY L. CARLSON
RITA SCHWEITZ

MOODY PRESS

CHICAGO

ISBN: 0-8024-2834-7

1 3 5 7 9 10 8 6 4 2

Printed in the United States of America

Contents

How to Use This Workbook

Sometimes we wonder if reading a book or working through a study guide can really make a difference. Randy Carlson was recently reminded of the value and power the principles found in this discovery journal can have in the life of any individual who desires personal growth. This is what happened.

Dr. Kevin Leman and I had just completed a weekend seminar attended by over 1,500 people in Michigan. The seminar had gone well, but we were physically and emotionally worn out and glad to be on our way home. As I collapsed into my assigned seat for the return flight to Tuscon, I noticed an attractive young woman step close to my seat. The woman I'll call Diane pulled a copy of my book *Father Memories* from her bag. "Are you Randy Carlson?" she asked.

"I certainly am."

Diane touched the book softly and smiled. "Thank you for writing *Father Memories*," she began. "I did what you said to do in the book, and it has revolutionized the relationship I've had—or should I say haven't had—with my father."

I returned her smile and encouraged her to continue. "Tell me about it."

"For the past fifteen years my father and I have had a bad relationship. I had almost given up hope of ever being close. Whenever I tried to tell him how I felt, the wall would go up and communication was over."

Diane went on to tell me how she used understanding gained from her father memories to break through the wall. "It was incredible," she said, her eyes misting up. "My husband and I are on our way home from visiting my dad. And we have an entirely new relationship. In fact, we ended the weekend with me crying my eyes out as I sat in my father's lap—something I've longed to do for fifteen years. Sharing with Dad my early father memories, and what they meant to me, opened everything up. We talked together in the way I've always wanted."

Diane rubbed her hand across the book again and swallowed hard. "Thanks again for writing this book. You can't begin to know all that it has meant to my father and me."

I thanked Diane for sharing her story with me; it lifted my spirits and made the remainder of the flight a great joy.

Like Diane, you can supplement Randy's book *Father Memories: How to discover the unique, powerful, and lasting impact your father has on your adult life and relationships* with the material and exercises in this workbook to rebuild a broken relationship. These exercises can also strengthen a good relationship or offer a new perspective on an unchangeable situation with your dad.

Completing this journal will be a valuable, life-changing experience even if you have not read *Father Memories*. But reading *Father Memories* before you start the exercises in this workbook, or reading *Father Memories* at the same time as you work through this material, will enhance your insights into yourself and your father.

The Bible talks of God's desire to "turn the hearts of the fathers to their children, and the hearts of the children to their fathers."[1] Diane has seen it happen. So can you.

But even if your relationship with your earthly father is not mended, you can draw closer to your Father in heaven. You were created in His image to love and enjoy Him. May God bless your efforts as you work through the following activities.

Writing as a Maturity Tool

People throughout the world and across many centuries have used writing as a way to express themselves and to get in touch with the deepest of human emotions. Often the writing had creative focus, resulting in beautiful poems, song lyrics, and literature. More often the diary or journal was quietly reflective; used to record significant happenings, chart the course, and mark the progress of one's private journey of discovery and personal growth. The therapeutic value of writing to vent frustration, quell anxiety, and share deep feelings has gained increasing attention by educators and psychologists in our generation. It works.

Writing things out works on both a personal and practical level. Management and business books have emphasized writing down pros and cons for decision making. Putting things down on paper forces you to clarify your thoughts and focus your concentration. Studies have shown that having a written business plan and clear goals set down in print greatly increases your chances of success. Some of the exercises we've included are intended to stimulate your own thinking in these ways. Other exercises are less analytical and may feel most natural for individuals who are more artistically inclined. We've tried to include a mix of creative and interactive exercises you can adapt to fit your needs, regardless of your personality and personal preferences.

Although we are going to give a few suggestions regarding the use of the exercises in this book, it is important to let the writing and insights speak specifically to your own experience. If the questions we ask miss the issue most significant to you, feel free to adapt or ignore it. This is your journal. *There is no right or wrong way to complete these exercises.* With that in mind, here are some brief tips that will help make your personal writing pleasant and rewarding:

- You don't have to let others read everything you've written. It can be scary to share your deepest hurts or fears with others. If the thought of having someone else read what you write will keep you from being completely honest, open, and uncensored, then it would be best to keep this journal confidential. Don't let the risk of sharing limit your efforts. God is willing to work with you in private; the important thing is that you feel safe enough to start.

- On the other hand, if your spouse, counselor, or trusted friend will respect what you're doing and help support you in the process of working through memories, then you may benefit from a compassionate listener. Sometimes an objective friend can help you make sense of your thoughts and feelings. Several topics in this journal could prompt profitable discussions and draw you close to others. The choice is yours.

- If you chose to share your feelings or show what you've written for any of the sections with your spouse, friend, parents, or counselor, simply let them read what you wrote or tell them what you feel. Don't apologize or justify or pretend it really doesn't matter that much.

- No editors or spell checkers allowed! Don't worry about using perfect grammar, punctuation, and complete sentences. Nobody, including yourself, needs to evaluate the quality of your prose. That is not the point. If you are embarrassed by your inability to spell words correctly, we can identify. Because we know first-hand how intimidating and inhibiting it can be to write when you don't spell well, we want you to set aside your dictionaries and past school scoldings. We encourage you not to worry about making mistakes. If *you* can understand what you meant to say, that's good enough.

- Developing skills and healthy habits takes time. You may feel desperate and want quick relief—you plan to zip through the workbook and get it over with. Yet deep down you already know it seldom works that way. What's the rush? Despite the pressure of our quick-fix, easy-answer society, healing of past hurts and growing toward wholeness is a process. Strong feelings will naturally arise as you work through your father memories, but there is no time pressure to settle everything today. We recommend that you use these exercises as a framework for your thoughts, a means to gain insight and principles for healthy living, not as a search for clear-cut explanations and immediate solutions. Take your time, pray, breath easy.

Consider your feelings.

- How did it feel to buy this workbook? To begin working in it? Are you curious? Expectant? A little nervous?

- What feelings are evoked by the phrase "father memories"?

- Do you work best on your own or with help? Don't worry about whether your choice makes sense to someone else; do what feels most comfortable for you.

Dad from the Grave

If your father is dead you will need to be aware of certain dynamics that will affect you as you work through these exercises. Check any tendencies you need to be aware of:

☐ *Touching Up the Family Portrait*

First, there is a common taboo in our culture: *Don't speak ill of the dead.* Because it is now impossible for you to speak to your father face to face, you may sense a feeling of censorship over any thoughts that might cast him in a negative light when he can't defend himself by telling his side of the story. It is not disloyal to remember things as they were rather than how you wished they would have been. Try to be honest in assessing your father's strengths and weaknesses as they relate to your response to life today. You may want to keep some of your thoughts to yourself, and that's fine, as long as you look at reality rather than a touched-up family portrait.

☐ *Selective Memory*

Even when we desire to be honest our memories have a way of highlighting the close times with loved ones we have lost. Dad's memory may be connected with a better, more secure, happier family life, especially if Dad died during our childhood. This is perfectly natural and healthy, provided Dad doesn't take on a hero's halo. Somehow in death a father may take on a "bigger than life" character. Try to select a balanced portfolio of memories, not just the wonderful moments.

☐ *The Cover-Up*

If you had a destructive or abusive relationship with your dad, it is important for you to internalize this message: "I am not responsible for the painful events in my childhood that stemmed from my father's sin. I let go of his responsibility." It is common for abused children to carry self-destructive "secrets" to protect a parent. We encourage you to bring everything out in the open. But be aware of the opposition: A common denominator in dysfunctional families is a joint conspiracy to cover up family problems, even to the degree of distorting history or reality.

☐ *Middle Men and Women*

If your father is no longer living you may have heard your mother, or a sibling, say something like "How do you think your father would feel if he saw the way you're acting?" or "I know you want to do what would make your father proud." Avoid triangles. Beware of accepting the pronouncements of a go-between regarding your father's view of what is being done. No one can or should be interpreting your relationship with your father or using his inferred approval or disapproval to manipulate your feelings and behavior.

☐ *Guided from the Grave*

On a positive note, it is possible to make peace with your father even if he isn't here to continue a relationship. Many adults have been comforted, guided, and reassured by the legacy of love their father left them. By making the most of your memories you can make the most of your life. Regardless of whether your dad is living or deceased, you hold the key to your own life. You can move on in life knowing that you are not alone; your Father in Heaven is still at your side.

Who Is Your Father?

Throughout this workbook we will be using the words "dad" or "father" to refer to the primary male caregiver in your childhood. Stepfathers, grandfathers, or older brothers who stepped into the father role qualify in the intent of the questions you will be asked. If you were adopted, you may choose to focus primarily on the active relationship with the father who raised you rather than the role of your biological father—adoption is a beautiful analogy of being welcomed into the family of God.

We also address our relationship with our Father in heaven. The Bible says that each of us is created in the image of God: "God created man in his own image, in the image of God he created him; male and female he created them."[2] God also invites us to become His children through a special adoption: "His unchanging plan has always been to adopt us into His own family by sending Jesus Christ to die for us. And He did this because He wanted to!"[3]

We become a part of God's family by faith, not by anything we do to deserve it. When we believe in Jesus as our Savior, we accept God's invitation to adopt us. But not everyone welcomes Jesus or accepts God's offer to be a loving Father. "Even in his own land and among his own people, the Jews, [Jesus] was not accepted. Only a few would welcome and receive him. But to all who received him, he gave the right to become children of God. All they needed to do was to trust him to save them."[4]

If you want to be a child of God but have never accepted God's offer of adoption, we encourage you to pray the following prayer. You can, of course, talk to God in your own words and invite Him to become your Father.

Dear God, I need the loving care and kindness you offer your children. I want to become your child, and I undestand that you eagerly adopt everyone who believes in Jesus. I know my sins have separated me from you, and I am trusting Jesus to bring us together again now by forgiving my sin. Thank you for giving me a place to belong and being a loving Father I can turn to.

If your heart is aching and you are trying to fill a father void in your heart, we especially encourage you to accept God's offer to help. For God is "a father to the fatherless. . . . God makes a home for the lonely."[5]

Part One

YOUR FATHER MEMORIES

What Do You Recall?

In a few moments you will be asked to write down some of your earliest memories with your father. In *Father Memories* (chapter 2), Randy offers a few pointers that will make the process easier and more profitable. Here is a summary of his suggestions:

- Father memories are full of the emotions you had as a little child—you shouldn't worry about editing them through adult eyes. Simply write down what happened and how you felt.

- The emotion tied to the memory and your perception of the incident are as important as the event itself. Try to write down not only what happened but how you responded and felt. What made an impression on you?

- Use your memories for improving yourself, not for blaming someone else.

- Try to recall your earliest and most vivid memories. If possible, try to go back before the age of eight.

As you fill in the following exercise, any memories will work. It doesn't have to be a major event or traumatic experience. Be sure to write down your own memory and not just a story you've been told by others. Try to list five or six father memories, starting with your earliest memory first. A general format is provided to help you as you write:

Father Memory #1   My approximate age: _____

I remember _____

_____

_____

_____

The clearest part of my memory is _____

_____

_____

As I think about the memory I feel _____

_____

_____

Father Memory #2   My approximate age: _____

I remember _____

_____

_____

_____

The clearest part of my memory is _____

_____

_____

As I think about the memory I feel _____

_____

_____

Father Memory #3   My approximate age: _____

I remember _____

_____

_____

_____

The clearest part of my memory is _____

_____

_____

As I think about the memory I feel _____

_____

_____

Father Memory #4   My approximate age: _____

I remember _____

_____

_____

_____

The clearest part of my memory is _____

_____

_____

_____

As I think about the memory I feel _____

_____

_____

Father Memory #5   My approximate age: _____

I remember _____

_____

_____

The clearest part of my memory is _____

_____

As I think about the memory I feel _____

_____

_____

Father Memory #6   My approximate age: _____

I remember _____

_____

_____

The clearest part of my memory is _____

_____

As I think about the memory I feel _____

_____

_____

Father Memory #7   My approximate age: _____

I remember _____

_____

_____

The clearest part of my memory is _____

_____

_____

As I think about the memory I feel _____

_____

_____

You will be asked to refer back to these memories in later exercises. But before you go on, note any insights or thoughts that came to mind while you wrote.

_____

_____

_____

_____

Do You Feel Depressed About Your Past?

On a flight returning from Washington, D.C., Rita happened to be seated by a corporate lawyer we'll call Sandra. Sandra and Rita began talking about Sandra's work, and it soon became evident that she had been under tremendous stress over the past nine months due to an attempted buy-out on the part of a competitive megacompany. The opposing team of attorneys had given Sandra an especially hard time because she was younger than the others and the only female.

"One man in particular treated me with disrespect. He reminded me so much of my father I could hardly stand to look at him!" Sandra blurted out.

It was clear that Sandra's childhood still hurt her, and it was natural for Rita to talk about some of the concepts contained in this journal. "You seem so calm now. How did you manage?"

"I didn't," Sandra said quietly. "My depression was out of control. I could not have helped myself. My husband insisted I see a doctor—the smartest thing I've ever done. Dr. M. put me on an antidepressant that saved my career, probably my life. Without the medication I couldn't concentrate or think straight enough to make the decisions that needed to be made. With the medication my life did a 180 degree turn in two weeks! Tell your readers that they don't have to feel miserable and desperate; there is a time to get medical help."

Sandra made an extremely important point. Some emotional and mental states are induced by chemical imbalances in the brain and nervous system. When this occurs, the individual needs prompt medical attention from a competent professional. Before you begin an aerobic exercise program you are advised to consult your physician and take a complete physical. Then, if necessary, the program can be monitored closely by your doctor to prevent harmful side effects or stress to the body. In a similar way, it is wise to recognize that the emotional and psychological make-up of the human body God designed is complex and worthy of respect. If you are struggling emotionally, right now may not be a safe time to tamper with disturbing memories without help from a trained therapist.

But since everyone gets depressed now and then, how do you know when it is wise to seek help? The following checklist is designed to indicate clinical depression requiring medical attention. It is adapted directly from the American Psychiatric Association's *Diagnostic and Statistical Manual of Mental Disorders. If at least five of the following symptoms have been present during the same two-week period, please consult your doctor before you proceed in this journal.*

Check any statement that is true of you:

☐ I feel depressed or am in an irritable mood most of the day, nearly every day.

☐ I have less interest or pleasure in activities. I find myself feeling apathetic toward the work and pursuits that were previously interesting to me.

☐ I have experienced significant weight loss or weight gain (when not dieting).

☐ I have trouble with sleep disturbances—either I sleep too much or too little. (One of the most prominent indicators of clinical depression is a disruption in the sleep cycle where one wakes at 3:00 or 4:00 in the morning and is not able to fall back asleep.)

☐ I've noticed sluggish body movement and slowed down muscle coordination. Or I feel physically restless or fidgety.

☐ Nearly every day, I feel fatigue or loss of energy that is not directly connected to my exertion. (This could be considered a normal reaction to the death of a loved one or other traumatic loss.)

☐ I'm more indecisive than usual; I have less ability to think or concentrate. And I am preoccupied with feelings of worthlessness or guilt.

☐ I have recurrent thoughts of death. I find myself thinking:
> "I wish I could go to sleep and never wake up."
> "I wish I could go away and never come back."
> "I'm ready to give up on life."[1]

Thank you for taking time to complete this mini-checkup. If at any time you become aware of these symptoms over a prolonged period, we encourage you to seek help to speed the healing process. Though for most individuals the process of exploring memories is empowering and rewarding, some persons find the strong feelings evoked by their memories very threatening. If at any time you think you would feel more comfortable talking things through with the support of a therapist, we encourage you to enlist the help of a qualified Christian counselor. Pray about your choice and seek out someone who is easy for you to confide in and who gives counsel you trust.

Like Father, Like Son . . . Like Father, Like Daughter?

There are many ways in which children may grow up to closely resemble their fathers. The genetic ties may result in similar body height, weight, and appearance. There may also be a similarity in temperament; for example, both may be outgoing, easily adapt to change, and enjoy adventure. Other likenesses may result from the manner in which the child is brought up and the model set by the father. The child may learn to be hard working, honest, and cheerful, like dad.

To identify several ways in which you are made in your father's image, quickly work through the following exercises. The first checklist deals with physical characteristics. Obviously, if you are a woman, you will need to make gender allowances as you consider some of the following.

My father and I have the same
- ☐ eye color
- ☐ hair color
- ☐ skin color
- ☐ facial appearance
- ☐ health problems
- ☐ body size and bone structure
- ☐ weight and muscle build
- ☐ _____
- ☐ _____

Like my father, I
- ☐ am athletic
- ☐ am nonathletic
- ☐ need little sleep
- ☐ need regular sleep
- ☐ am allergic to certain things
- ☐ have good eyesight
- ☐ have poor eyesight
- ☐ _____
- ☐ _____

Now think of twenty ways you could complete the following sentence:

"My father _____, and so do I."

For instance: My father *works hard,* and so do I.
My father *loves music,* and so do I.
My father *gets stubborn sometimes,* and so do I.
My father *distrusts politicians,* and so do I.

My father _____, and so do I.

My father _____, and so do I.

My father _____, and so do I.

My father _____, and so do I.

My father _____, and so do I.

My father _____, and so do I.

My father _____, and so do I.

My father _____, and so do I.

My father _____, and so do I.

My father _____, and so do I.

My father _____, and so do I.

My father _____, and so do I.

My father _____, and so do I.

My father _____, and so do I.

My father _____, and so do I.

My father _____, and so do I.

My father _____, and so do I.

My father _____, and so do I.

My father _____, and so do I.

My father _____, and so do I.

God designed families such that fathers should take an active interest in the training of their children. It is healthy and natural for a youngster to want to grow up to be "just like Dad." The exercises above should have given you a clue regarding the ways your values, abilities, behavior, and lifestyle have been influenced by your father. If your father was a man of good character, you have a privileged heritage, and it is a blessing to follow in his footsteps. But such is not always the case, as is poignantly communicated in the song "The Cat's In the Cradle," wherein the father finally recognizes his lifelong failings and sadly notes that his son has grown up just like him.

I believe my parents were responsible for what they did then; I am responsible for what I do now.

Lee Ezell[2]

Sometimes the father's influence is seen in counter-control, a sort of rebound effect. For example, an adult son or daughter may reason along these lines:

"My father was stingy with his money, so I determined I would make more money and be generous when I grew up."

"My father was kind to a fault, and I decided I didn't want to let others take advantage of me."

"My father played favorites, and I vowed I would never do that to my kids."

The perceptions of your father and his motives may not be accurate, but they exert influence over your behavior as if they were. Can you think of areas where the deliberate desire to be different from your father is controlling your behavior? If so, list them here:

_____

_____

_____

_____

_____

_____

The Broad Strokes of Your Background

In *Family Matters,* Daniel Gottlieb talks about understanding our memories in the context of a painting. He writes, "Broad strokes are placed on those portraits-of-the-world by our early experiences, both with our parents and with our loved ones. Peers and other significant people add further brush strokes. For most of us, the paint dries early."[3]

Sit down at a table when you can have at least a half hour or longer of uninterrupted time. Write down what you feel are the most significant aspects of your relationship with your father. In this brief overview look for the broad strokes in your background, both light and dark, that have shaped your relationship. Don't worry about what everything means or try to figure out why you select particular things and not others. This is just a basic summary, so don't get bogged down in detail.

_____

_____

_____

_____

_____

_____

_____

_____

_____

_____

_____

_____

_____

_____

_____

_____

_____

_____

Now that you have finished jotting down some thoughts about your relationship with your father, answer the following questions:

Do you consider that your childhood was complete? ☐ Yes ☐ No

If so, why? Or if not, what was missing? _____

_____

_____

_____

_____

If you could change the time you spent with your father, what would you change?

_____

_____

_____

_____

_____

What would you leave the same—or add? _____

_____

_____

_____

How would you change the way he acted or reacted toward you as a child? _____

_____

_____

Would you change the way your father treats you now? ☐ Yes ☐ No

What would you like to change? _____

_____

_____

_____

If your father could change anything about your relationship during your childhood, what do you think he would wish were different? _____

_____

_____

_____

Do you think he would want to change any of the ways you act or react now?

☐ Yes ☐ No

If so, what? _____

_____

_____

Can you think of anything God would like to see changed in your relationship with your dad? ☐ Yes ☐ No

If so, what? _____

_____

_____

What Do You Hope to Accomplish?

It always helps to be moving toward a definite goal. As you work through these exercises, what do you hope to accomplish? _____

_____

_____

_____

_____

What role, if any, does your father play in this desire? _____

_____

_____

_____

What do you hope God will do to help you? _____

_____

_____

_____

The Past Is History. What Can You Do About It?

When you were young and growing up, your thinking and attitudes about life were shaped by your experience and interaction with your father and mother. As an adult, what can you do about the things that happened in the past? The following exercises are designed to help you

- ✔ sort out some of those fuzzy memories, and make sense of what you do remember clearly.

- ✔ increase your understanding of the times and ways your father memories influence your life today.

- ✔ work through to a better relationship with your dad, men, authority figures, and heavenly Father.

- ✔ accept and make the most of your memories.

Understanding the Foundation Your Father Set

Good parenting is built on the basics of dependability, consistency, and security. In the book *Father Memories* (pages 18-29), Randy wrote about five foundations of healthy fathers. Consider how dependable and consistent your father was in modeling and verbalizing each of those five key areas. The purpose of the evaluation is simply to discover more about your foundation for life, not to pass judgment or place blame. Circle the number rating that you feel best describes the degree to which your father provided these things.

1. *Did your father provide emotional security?*

0	1	2	3	4	5	6	7	8	9	10
Never		Very Seldom			Some of the Time			Almost Always		Consistently

2. *Did your father value you as a person?*

0	1	2	3	4	5	6	7	8	9	10
Never		Very Seldom			Some of the Time			Almost Always		Consistently

3. *Did your father teach you healthy touching and offer physical affection?*

0	1	2	3	4	5	6	7	8	9	10
Never		Very Seldom			Some of the Time			Almost Always		Consistently

4. *Did your father set boundaries and enforce them with consistent discipline?*

0	1	2	3	4	5	6	7	8	9	10
Never		Very Seldom			Some of the Time			Almost Always		Consistently

5. *Did your father teach you right values and help you build a belief system that leads to wise, balanced, and moral living?*

0	1	2	3	4	5	6	7	8	9	10
Never		Very Seldom			Some of the Time			Almost Always		Consistently

How you answer these five questions reflects, to a large degree, the kind of foundation upon which your early life rested. And a shaky foundation can affect the rest of a person's life. There are, of course, ways to compensate for certain deficiencies in order to provide a strong upbringing. The most obvious method of compensation is the unique way in which a husband and wife complement each other as a parenting team. This is God's design, and we do not wish to imply that any one man should manage every area with perfect consistency. No person could.

How you chose to answer may also reveal a great deal about how you are dealing with emotional conflicts today. Think carefully as you work through the next section.

Foundation One: Emotional Security

Let's back up and explore more deeply how the answers to the five questions above impact your life today. To begin, did your father provide emotional security? If so, in what way? If not, how do you know? Write down some examples from your father memories:

_____

_____

_____

_____

_____

_____

_____

_____

How do you think your life would be different today if your answer had been the opposite? (If you had the emotional security you lacked; or if you lacked the emotional security he provided.) _____

_____

_____

_____

_____

_____

Emotional security is an essential part of the foundation to a healthy life. Without it a person feels like he or she is walking on quicksand; any moment the bottom could give way and they would be dangerously out of control. Lack of security in childhood sets up the child for insecurity in adulthood. Insecure adults make a big deal about staying in *control*.

Is it important for you to be in control?_____

_____

_____

Do you feel threatened by change? _____

_____

_____

When you are not in control of a situation or person, how do you feel?_____

_____

_____

_____

_____

Think of the last time you were not in control. How did you respond to the situation?

_____

_____

_____

_____

Being vulnerable and open with others requires an ability to give up control and trust. At what times is it hard for you to be vulnerable with other people? Why?_____

_____

_____

_____

Do you think you maintain balance in this area of life, opening up to "safe" people and keeping firm boundaries with those you are less close to? _____

_____

_____

_____

Is it hard for you to give up control to God? Give an example or two to support your answer. ☐ Yes ☐ Sometimes ☐ No

Examples: _____

_____

_____

_____

_____

The Bible encourages, "Cast all your anxiety on [God] because he cares for you."[1] And Psalm 46:1 tells us that "God is our refuge and strength, an ever-present help in trouble." Does God "feel" like a refuge and strength in life? ☐ Yes ☐ Sometimes ☐ No

If so, in what ways? _____

_____

_____

Did your dad feel like a support and strength to you as a child? ☐ Yes ☐ Sometimes ☐ No

Look for correlations between your perception of your dad and your feelings toward God. Are they similar? ☐ Yes ☐ No

Why or why not? _____

_____

_____

NOTE: Never base biblical acceptance on feelings alone. The fact is, God remains a refuge and strength whether you feel it or not. Because feelings are so easily influenced by past experience, present mood, and physical condition, always be wary of trusting your feelings. Never trust them if they violate scriptural truth.

Feeling Emotionally Secure:
What things did your father do when you were a child that made you feel secure?

_____

_____

_____

What did he do that made you feel insecure? _____

_____

_____

_____

What things do your spouse (or boss) do that make you feel secure? _____

_____

_____

_____

Insecure? _____

_____

_____

List any similarities between your father's actions and those of your present employer or spouse.

_____

_____

_____

Does your sense of emotional security fluctuate due to events you experience, or does it remain constant? _____

What makes you say so? _____

_____

_____

_____

Foundation Two—Where You Valued by Your Father?

Did your father value you as a person? ☐ Yes ☐ No

Give an example or two that supports your answer: _____

_____

_____

_____

_____

Deep emotional wounds can occur if the love and affection we extended to our fathers were not reciprocated the way we hoped they would be. By contrast, mutual love and respect equip a child to face life feeling secure, valued, and whole. Check each of the following statements that was true of your relationship with your father when you were a child:

- ☐ I loved my father, and he loved me.
- ☐ I trusted my father, and he trusted me.
- ☐ I appreciated my father, and he appreciated me.
- ☐ I enjoyed being with my father, and he enjoyed being with me.
- ☐ I respected my father, and he respected me.
- ☐ I listened to my father, and he listened to me.
- ☐ I was proud of my father, and he was proud of me.
- ☐ I _____ my father, and he _____ me.
- ☐ I _____ my father, and he _____ me.
- ☐ I _____ my father, and he _____ me.

Can you think of a time you offered affection or respect to your dad when he didn't respond as you hoped? _____

_____

_____

_____

Why do you think he failed to respond? _____

_____

_____

_____

How did that make you feel at the time? _____

_____

_____

_____

How do you feel about it now? _____

_____

_____

_____

Can you think of a time when your father's loving response was especially meaningful to you?

_____

_____

Why? _____

_____

When we love God we never have to worry about Him loving us back—God loved us *first!* "We love because he first loved us."[2] God always provides a constant stream of respect, kindness, affection, and love for His children. Even a heart left aching from childhood can be filled with God's compassion and healed by His tender care.

See God as your perfect parent. Sit back, close your eyes, and imagine yourself climbing into God's lap and resting against Him. Soak in the security, comfort, and love you feel in His arms. If your earthly father was sexually or physically abusive, or hard and distant toward you, you may find it easier to emotionally connect to the mother-heart of God. In the Bible God says His love is like that of both fathers and mothers for their children: "As a mother comforts her child, so will I comfort you"; "you saw how the Lord your God carried you, as a father carries his son, all the way you went until you reached this place."[3] Visualize God actually carrying you or comforting you until these verses become real to your heart. How does it feel to imagine the intimate love of God?

_____

_____

_____

A grateful heart

As you worked through these exercises, you may have been reminded of several things you appreciate about the fathering you received. Have you ever said ''thank you'' to your father for the time and love he invested in your life? Parenting is often a thankless task, and receiving a letter or call from you expressing your appreciation may mean a lot to your father. You might also want to thank your Father in heaven for your childhood home and family. It is good to give thanks from a grateful heart.

The need to feel valued and cared for is God given. And if that need is not met early in life, a void develops. Acting out, withdrawing from others, or feeling an emptiness inside are typical symptoms of a child or adult trying to fill that void. Understanding what God says about your value to Him—He loved you so much He sent His Son to die for your sins—can help heal the hurt. But we also want to feel valued and needed by our loved ones here on earth.

Do you feel valued by others today? ☐ Yes ☐ No

In what ways? _____

_____

_____

_____

How do you show others that they are valuable? Write out specific ways.

1. _____
2. _____
3. _____
4. _____
5. _____

If you do not feel valued and cherished, God knows about that too. He understands and cares. It is very helpful to memorize and meditate on Psalm 103:13 when you feel blue: "As a father has compassion on his children, so the Lord has compassion on those who fear him." Writing this verse three times in the blanks provided will help you learn and remember it.

_____

_____

_____

_____

_____

If you don't feel valuable to others, you likely don't feel valuable to yourself either. We each must discipline our thoughts and bring our feelings about ourselves into line with the truth: _We are valuable!_ Put a check next to each of the following statements that is true for you:

☐ I know what I'm good at in life, and I'm doing it.
☐ I feel that my thoughts and opinions are important and are to be respected.
☐ If I died today, I would be missed.
☐ I have goals in life that I'm working to accomplish.
☐ I value the contribution I can make to my family, church, and community.
☐ I take good care of my body.
☐ I value myself enough to take care of my appearance.
☐ I understand that my value does not rest upon what others think of me.

If you put a check by most of the above statements, congratulations. If you couldn't do that, then you have specific areas where your work is cut out for you. No one can change your attitude about yourself but you. And with God's help you can challenge any lies of unworthinesss you may have picked up in childhood.

Foundation Three: Healthy Touching

Touching is one of the most intimate forms of communication. The manner in which we touch each other can communicate anything from love to anger, affection to rejection, sympathy to superiority. Nonverbal communication was an important part of your relationship with your father. For example, a tender touch may have moved you toward closeness while rough touches created distance and hurt feelings.

Did you grow up in a family that physically expressed their love through hugs, kisses, or arms around the shoulders? ☐ Yes ☐ No

As you think about your father memories, give an example that you remember of healthy touching: _____

_____

_____

In our society an alarming number of children are sexually or physically abused. If you experienced trauma as a child, this entire section may be very painful. (Note: If you discover the level of anger or pain rising as you work through this section, we recommend that you skip over it for now and seek out a professional Christian counselor for help.)

Can you recall being touched in a way that you didn't like?

_____

_____

_____

Types of Touch You Are Comfortable With:
Giving and receiving affection is a normal part of life, but families have different comfort zones for physical interaction. Check the types of touch you were most comfortable giving and receiving as a child, then check the right-hand column to indicate the way you feel now.

THEN:			NOW:	
Giving/Receiving			Giving/Receiving	
☐	☐	hugs	☐	☐
☐	☐	kisses	☐	☐
☐	☐	handshakes	☐	☐
☐	☐	holding hands	☐	☐
☐	☐	tickles and playful wrestling	☐	☐
☐	☐	sitting close or in a lap	☐	☐
☐		arm around the shoulder	☐	☐

Where are you on the giving and taking continuum? Circle the degree to which you like friends and family members to express themselves by touching you.

1	2	3	4	5	6	7	8	9	10
Don't Touch				It's OK					Please Touch

Now circle how free you feel about touching others.

1	2	3	4	5	6	7	8	9	10
Don't Touch				It's OK					Please Touch

Now go back on each scale and put a box around the number that represents where you would like to be.

Physical Affection in Marriage:

Touching is an important part of marriage. Many couples run into big problems because they have differences over the amount and type of sexual and nonsexual touch they prefer. If you are married, work toward open communication in this area.

Is it difficult for you to talk to your spouse about what touching you like and don't like?
☐ Yes ☐ No

What bothers you and what pleases you most about the physical expressions of love in your marriage? _____

_____

_____

_____

How has this affected your marriage? _____

_____

_____

_____

Foundation Four: Boundaries and Discipline

Agreed upon boundaries protect and preserve peace. That's true for countries and true for individuals.

Did your father set boundaries and enforce them with consistent discipline? ☐ Yes
☐ No

What were some of the boundaries and rules you grew up with? _____

_____

_____

_____

_____

_____

If you have children of your own, do they have the same rules you grew up with? ☐ Yes ☐ No

Why or why not? _____

_____

_____

_____

Who set the limits and rules in your family when you were a child? _____

How easily could the rules be bent or broken? _____

_____

How were those rules enforced? _____

_____

_____

Did you feel that those in authority over you were fair? ☐ Yes ☐ No

Why? _____

_____

_____

Do you think that this past experience influences your expectations and respect for those in authority now (your boss, pastor, governmental and law enforcement personnel)? ☐ Yes ☐ No

In what ways do you think it sometimes affects your response or outlook? _____

_____

_____

_____

Boundaries, Self-Discipline, and Protection:

As adults we are generally called upon to exercise self-discipline—that is, to make and hold ourselves to certain standards. When a child lives under fair and consistent discipline, he learns to internalize standards and discipline himself without derogatory self-accusations or destructive self-punishment. By contrast, children who learn a rebellious hatred for mean or unjust discipline often have a difficult time learning mature self-discipline and coming under the just authority of God.

The following list contains several key areas of life. Next to each area write out what boundaries you have set for yourself and how those boundaries have protected you. If you don't have limits in certain areas, write out what boundaries you are willing to set and how you will hold yourself accountable.

For example, under "relationships with the opposite sex" Randy has set this boundary: "I will not encourage or develop a friendship with a woman unless my wife is part of that friendship (boundary). And if I need to spend time with a woman alone for business purposes my wife is always the first to know (accountability)."

The following are my boundaries and accountability for:

Money
    Boundaries: _____

    _____

    Accountability: _____

    _____

Diet
    Boundaries: _____

    _____

    Accountability: _____

    _____

Work
    Boundaries: _____

    _____

    Accountability: _____

    _____

Friendships
    Boundaries: _____

    _____

    Accountability: _____

    _____

Expressing emotions (anger, discouragement, affection, and so on)
    Boundaries: _____

    _____

    Accountability: _____

    _____

Relationships with the opposite sex
    Boundaries: _____

    _____

    Accountability: _____

    _____

Church involvement
  Boundaries: _____

  _____

  Accountability: _____

  _____

Consider the protection each limit provides. Individuals who exercise self-restraint actually enjoy a much greater degree of personal freedom and satisfaction than those who impose no limits on their own behavior. In the same way, persons who choose to live under the laws of God find protection and avoid heartaches that often result from undisciplined behavior.

Foundation Five: Values

Values form the inner grid that screens our decision-making process. Values develop on the inside and work their way out through every aspect of our life. What kinds of values do you remember your father instilling in your life? From your father memories write out an example or phrase that would reflect what your dad taught you about each of the following:

Devotion to God _____

Love for others _____

Respect for authority _____

Use and importance of money _____

Self-discipline and self-control _____

Obedience to God's commandments _____

The importance of feelings _____

Patriotism and voting _____

Humbleness of spirit _____

Attitude toward employment _____

Chapter 11 ("What Dad Did Right") in *Father Memories* discusses the need for a balanced look at both the positive and negative side of the parenting you received. Too often in therapy or self-evaluation, there is an inappropriate focus on everything that was wrong without equal consideration of how to make the most of what was right about our past. The following exercises give you the opportunity to look at the positive aspects of your past and build on them.

Credit Where Credit Is Due:
What character qualities are your areas of strength? _____

_____

What do you like about yourself? _____

_____

_____

Chances are, the seeds of your successes and strengths were planted in your childhood. So let's set aside this section to applaud all that your parents, especially your dad, did right. To get started, check the items below that were communicated to you through words or deeds during your childhood. Feel free to add to the list—the longer list the better!

My dad was

☐ a good provider   ☐ an encourager
☐ the spiritual head of our home   ☐ easy to talk to
☐ the leader of our family   ☐ consistent with discipline
☐ one of my best friends   ☐ concerned about me

My dad modeled or taught

☐ love and respect for your fellow man
☐ obedience to divine commandments
☐ self-discipline and self-control
☐ humbleness of spirit
☐ tenderness and compassion for those who hurt
☐ respect for authority
☐ wholehearted devotion to God
☐ love for your country
☐ that family is important—stay true to each other
☐ honesty—follow through on what you promise
☐ enthusiasm for life

Choosing Values:
After looking at the above lists, to what degree have you adopted your father's values as your own? _____

_____

_____

_____

Most of us, by habit, act on values we have not clearly thought through. How we use time, money, and things can be very revealing. Some of us who were blessed with a strong foundation from childhood can fly through life on "automatic pilot" and do pretty well. For others, the knee-jerk reaction in certain areas will always be wrong. Mike's father, for example valued extreme self-reliance, and Mike's automatic instict is *never, ever ask for help*. Like Mike, there will be areas in which you will need to question the values that drive your behavior, then make some changes. And there will be areas where you can build on the values you were taught as a child. Here are two suggestions to get you started:

1. *Strive to be principle driven.* Check all daily "to do" lists against what is truly important to you. You may find that you are doing certain things because you feel others expect you to or because that's the way it's always been done, rather than doing them because you feel they are the most valuable way to spend your time. Cross-examine your priorities in light of where you spend your time: "If I feel my family is more important than my career why do I spend evenings and weekends working instead of being them them?"

2. *Write out a personal mission statement.* Make it short and to the point, but include what is important to you. For example, as president of Today's Family Life, Randy Carlson wrote a mission statement for their ministry that clearly stated their values:

Today's Family Life Mission Statement

People first:

We believe that people are God's most valued creation. For God so loved the people of all generations, of all cultures, of all races, of all religions, that He sent His Son, Jesus Christ, to die for their sins. We believe that the mission of Today's Family Life, which is to restore and prevent broken relationships, is consistent with God's great love for the peoples of the world. . . .

Therefore, we all commit ourselves to creating and implementing individual and collective programs that will put:

People Before Systems
People Before Comfort
People Before Things
People Before Money
People Before Paperwork
People Before Daily Routine

"All hard work brings a profit, but mere talk leads only to poverty" (Proverbs 14:23).

Write your own mission statement here:

Personal Mission Statement

_____

_____

_____

_____

_____

_____

_____

_____

_____

_____

_____

_____

_____

_____

_____

_____

Part Two
MAKING THE MOST OF YOUR MEMORIES

Your Personal Perception

In their book *Unlocking the Secrets of Your Childhood Memories,* Kevin Leman and Randy Carlson explain the amazing way a person's earliest childhood memories give insight into a person's overall lifestyle.[1] We tend to remember most clearly those incidents that fit or are consistent with the way we see ourselves in relation to others and our world. Our father memories contain our own personal perception of life.

Refer back to your list of father memories on pages 15-18. Choose one memory to focus on first. What makes this memory stand out to you? _____

_____

_____

_____

_____

What is the dominant feeling you associate with this memory? _____

_____

_____

Working through this section will help you discover how early memories can indicate patterns in the life-script you are acting out, help you uncover any lies about life you tell yourself, and indicate faulty perceptions you act upon. Once you are aware of those lies and how they impact your life, you will be in a position to do something about them.

We see the world through distorted lenses—lenses of our own making. Others grind away at the lens, but as adults ultimately we make the choice (actively or by default) to see the world the way we do today. How do you see the world?

Based on your childhood memories, think of two words or phrases to complete the following:

I am _____

The world is _____

Others are _____

God is _____

Money is _____

Work is _____

Men are _____

Women are _____

Children are _____

Many of these beliefs were picked up early in life and stuck. Memories show positive seeds to our characters that were planted in our early years, as well as dangerous distortions and misbeliefs.

What is it about your father memories that bugs you the most? _____

_____

_____

_____

Does that thought impact your life today? ☐ Yes ☐ No

If yes, in what ways? _____

_____

Are your memories ☐ more or ☐ less troublesome today than one year ago?

The one thing about my father or father memories that I want to be free from is

_____

_____

_____

Perception Is the Key

The past is immovable, but your perceptions of it are like putty. Your present mood and current events can greatly color how you see the past. So let's focus on perceptions in this section with the understanding that the way you saw things as a child may not have been accurate, but it was still significant.

What one word comes to mind when you think about your father? _____

What one word would he use (or would have) to describe himself? _____

Our guess is they don't agree. Why? _____

_____

_____

_____

If you said that each person's experience influences his or her personal perception, we agree. Father memories are like snapshots of the past that are developed in our mind to reflect what's inside us today.

Think back to the dominant feeling you associated with the father memory you wrote down earlier. Does that feeling appear in any of your other memories? ☐ Yes ☐ No

How does that feeling fit the way you feel about life today? _____

_____

_____

_____

In what ways is the little boy or girl described in your memory consistent with the person you are today? _____

_____

_____

_____

There is a saying: Ask fish to describe their lives and they will forget to mention water.

For many individuals, the family environment was the "water" in which they swam, and they cannot see its effect on them because it is too great. It is the only "normal" they have ever known, and they have difficulty evaluating the overall tone, strengths, and weaknesses in their own home life. Because we all have blind spots, it may be helpful for you to have someone else listen to your father memories and make observations—they may see things your subjective eyes miss. Siblings, other family members, and childhood friends may also be able to help you gain a truer picture of your past and the factors that influenced your upbringing.

To help you explore further this concept of personal perception as revealed through your father memories, think about how the little person in those memories is still alive today. Check each statement that is true:

Memory	Adult Life
☐ I felt alone.	You are a loner, even in a crowd.
☐ I felt fear.	You worry about many things.
☐ Lots of detail.	You're a detail, detail, detail person.
☐ Color, smell, or touch.	You are creative.
☐ No feelings at all.	It's hard for you to sort out what you really feel today.

☐ I am active.　　　　　　　　You still are.
☐ I am passive.　　　　　　　You still tend to be passive and observe life.
☐ I felt safe.　　　　　　　　Security and safety are important to you today.
☐ I felt like I needed to please.　You don't want to rock the boat.
☐ I felt anger.　　　　　　　Anger is a problem today.

Take a moment and add to this list. Write out any patterns you observe.

☐ _____　_____
☐ _____　_____
☐ _____　_____

In Many Ways the Little Boy or Girl You Once Were, You Still Are

To continue on with this line of thinking, consider the correlation between your father memories and your relationship to him today (or when he was alive).

What place does your father take in your memories (close, distant, absent, etc.)? _____
_____

What is your relationship like with your dad today? _____
_____
_____

How does this impact other relationships? _____
_____
_____

What role or roles do you assume in your father memories? Check those that apply.

☐ I'm the black sheep.　　　　　☐ I'm the athletic one.
☐ I'm the good kid.　　　　　　☐ I'm the stubborn one.
☐ I'm the peacemaker.　　　　　☐ I'm the quiet one.
☐ I'm the rebellious one.　　　　☐ I'm the outsider.
☐ I'm the listening ear.　　　　　☐ I'm the baby in the family.

The lies we tell ourselves may be related to the roles we assumed or messages we internalized. These lies tend to move us away from what is good and toward destructive patterns. Can you think of any lies you are telling yourself?

Check those that apply:

☐ Life is unfair.　　　　　　☐ Confrontation is bad (or difficult).
☐ Others don't like me.　　　　☐ It's all my fault.

- [ ] I'm stupid.
- [ ] I must please others.
- [ ] I'm ugly.
- [ ] I'm clumsy.
- [ ] It's all my parent's fault.
- [ ] Food fills the emptiness I feel inside.
- [ ] No one will ever love me.
- [ ] If I had a different job I would be happy.
- [ ] _____
- [ ] _____
- [ ] _____

Changing Your Perception

Your faulty inner messages can make you bend to conformity, trying to be like others or please others rather than being yourself. Changing the destructive messages you tell yourself isn't like changing your clothes. It takes a great deal more insight, commitment, and prayer.

Get ready for a battle. For as you begin to challenge your thinking and break new paths of behavior the shortcut to fall back into old patterns of thinking lies around the corner. At the least resistance your heart and mind will begin wooing you back toward old patterns and more comfortable paths. Resist this temptation and press on. (For more discussion on uncovering and changing the lies in our memories, see pages 179-84 in *Father Memories*.)

We forfeit three-fourths of ourselves to be like—or be liked—by other people.

Take this section seriously. Move as slowly and prayerfully as necessary. First, write out in detail the one lie you most often tell yourself (perhaps from the list above). It may be subtle, such as "Only hard workers are worth much as people," or, "Men only pay attention to attractive women," yet it influences your choices.

The lie(s) I catch myself believing is (are) _____

_____

_____

_____

_____

_____

How has this lie kept you from reaching some of your heart's desires or goals in life?

_____

_____

_____

_____

How would your life be different today if you could change your thinking on just this one issue? (Would you feel less guilty, have more options, gain self-confidence, and so on?)

_____

_____

_____

How badly do you want to overcome the effects of this lie in your life?

1	2	3	4	5	6	7	8	9	10
Not really				Somewhat					Very Much

Here are some steps to help challenge the distortions in your perceptions and to help you begin telling yourself the truth:

1. *Next to the lie write out the truth.* For example, someone might write, "The lie is: Others won't love me if I don't conform to their standards. But the truth is: I don't have to give up being me in order to be loved by them."

The lie is: _____

But the truth is: _____

2. *Commit to memorizing Scripture that encourages the truth.* If you do not have another verse in mind, memorize Philippians 4:8. Look it up for yourself and speak it out loud as you write it down.

_____

_____

_____

3. *Ask a friend or family member to help hold you accountable* when he or she catches you telling yourself (and them by word, action, or look) the lie.

Who is the person you can trust to help hold you accountable? _____

What do you want them to say to you as a reminder? _____

_____

_____

Will you tell them they can feel free to confront you privately whenever necessary? ☐ Yes ☐ No

How do you see this exercise helping to improve your life? _____

_____

_____

_____

_____

Positive Character Traits You Have Learned

Here is a list of significant skills you may have learned. Go through the list quickly and underline those that are important to you. Then go back through the list putting a "D" next to those skills your dad possesses and your own initial for those you can see in yourself.

_____ *responsibility:* recognizing and doing your part

_____ *confidence:* feeling able to do it

_____ *initiative:* seeing what to do and moving into action

_____ *patience:* willing to wait when necessary

_____ *kindness:* showing caring concern for others

_____ *problem solving:* putting your knowledge and ability to use

_____ *integrity:* telling the truth and living out your convictions

_____ *teamwork:* working well with others

_____ *perseverence:* completing what you start

_____ *motivation:* wanting to do it

_____ *determination:* doing it when you don't want to

_____ *courage:* demonstrating the inner strength to act rightly in spite of fear

_____ *creativity:* coming up with new ways to say or do it

_____ *independence:* doing it on your own when necessary

_____ *supportiveness:* encouraging others to do their best

_____ *verbal:* expressing feelings and concerns

_____ *obedience:* respecting and submitting to authority

_____ *loving:* caring deeply for others

Whenever you find any of those traits in yourself, you have found the touch of God and the touch of love on your life. These are personal strengths you can make the most of in achieving your goals and serving the Lord in adult life.

Drawing Strength from the Past

Healthy people have the ability to take positive feelings of affirmation, love, support, and comfort from the past and introject them into the present for encouragement. Their memories become a source of strength to draw on when times get tough. R. C. Sproul, a noted and entertaining scholar who has written many books, recommends the following exercise and discusses the process, based on his personal experience:

> The organization which employs me once engaged the professional services of a management consultant. . . . His opening gambit was to raise the following question: "What are the five most meaningful compliments you've ever received?" The consultant handed me a pencil and a piece of paper and asked me to jot down in brief the five compliments that came to mind, noting from whom I had received them and at what point in my life they had come. I filled out the paper as instructed and was surprised by the things I discovered about myself and my life.[1]

Before we go on with his story, complete your own list of meaningful compliments here, using the directions above:

1. _____
_____
_____

2. _____
_____
_____

3. _____
_____
_____

4. _____
_____
_____

5. _____
_____
_____

"One of the five memorable compliments I wrote on the paper," Sproul continued, "came from my eighth-grade English teacher after completing a homework assignment. We had been instructed to write a descriptive paragraph, letting our imaginations roam freely as we made our virgin attempt at creative writing. When the papers were graded the teacher announced, 'Before I return these papers, there is one I want to read aloud.'

> To my unmitigated shock, she exposed to the ears of everyone in the class the content of my descriptive paragraph, and posted my paper on the bulletin board where everyone could see it. Few grasped the significance of that act for my dignity. The bulletin board was normally reserved for the display of the students' artwork. I was the poorest art student in the class and had the ignominious distinction of being the only student to never have had his artwork displayed on the bulletin board. In one fell swoop, I made the big time as my English composition was considered a work of art. After class, I went to the front of the room to gaze at the impossible, to stare at my trophy which carried me to the heights of glory. There, emblazoned on the margin, beneath the grade, were the words of my teacher, "R. C., don't ever let anyone tell you that you can't write."
>
> Do you have any idea how many people have since tried to tell me I cannot write? . . . My last book went through seven revisions before I submitted the final polished version. . . . When I received my manuscript back from the copy editor, however, it had so much red ink it looked like the balance sheet of the Chrysler Corporation. I don't know exactly how many marks there were on the manuscript, but I made a fair estimate. I counted the number of marks on the first ten pages and then figured an average for the entire manuscript. The estimate totaled approximately ten thousand critical marks. That should be enough to convince the most recalcitrant egomaniac that he ought to give up. But there they were, the words of my teacher, "Never let anyone tell you you can't write." And here I am again—writing my fool fingers off.[2]

Look back over your list of compliments. Have there been times when you needed those words to help keep you from giving up? Sproul explains that "we tend to treasure compliments given to us from people we esteem. If we respect the person who pays us a compliment, we will be more likely to cherish the praise and nurse it to our bosom. It will add steel to our brittle self-respect."[3] That is why the comments of a father, mother, coach, or boss carry extra weight, provided they are believable—flattery won't carry us far.

Go back through your list of most meaningful compliments. Consider ways you can build on these affirming words and use them to silence critical voices and self-doubts. Then do the exercise in reverse: fill in the five most painful insults you've ever received. Note who made the comment and when. Writing down these remarks may open old wounds, but it can also indicate ways in which your past is exercising negative control over your life.

1. _____

_____

_____

2. _____

3. _____

_____

_____

4. _____

_____

_____

5. _____

_____

_____

Notice that we did not put a time frame on the compliments or painful remarks you remembered. Although it is in vogue to talk about the hurt inner "child," it is more accurate to consider the inner "person." Adolescent adjustments, career choice, marriage and sexual experience, having a baby, or any major trauma can leave us emotionally vulnerable and pliable. How your father expresses support or withholds approval during these key times will impact your relationship. Often these events trigger change regardless of whether they occurred in early childhood.

Too often we listen to the wrong whispers from the past:

> "You're not good enough."
> "Nobody really likes you."
> "You're unattractive."

Instead, we need to replay those meaningful compliments and reassurances that remind us of our God-given dignity and worth. Because we are created in the image of our heavenly Father, we have the capacity to imagine and create. Imagination can be a very constructive force in the healing of memories.

Select one painful memory from the list above. Now imagine yourself reentering that memory with God at your side. What would your heavenly Father say to you at that moment to comfort and encourage you? What would you, as an adult, say to defend and love the child who is being insulted? To work through each memory, write two letters in the space provided. First, write a letter from the younger, hurt person you were when the insult occurred to the adult you are now, telling how it felt to experience that incident and what you desperately wanted from your father, your heavenly Father, or those around you.

Dear (adult) _____,

_____

_____

_____

_____

_____

_____

_____

_____

_____

_____

_____

_____

_____

Now write a letter to the child, young man, or young woman you once were from the adult you now are. Use the truth about God and life that you now know to comfort and counsel the hurt inner person from your memory. Imagine yourself as a competent adult walking into the memory and setting things straight.

Dear (young) _____,

_____

_____

_____

_____

_____

_____

_____

_____

_____

_____

_____

Pray about each of the painful memories from the past, asking God to heal those damaged emotions. If you experienced traumatic events that continue to haunt you, we recommend that you share them with a mature Christian who is able to give wise counsel.

Men, Women, and Memories

How you view the roles of men and women in the home and in society has roots in your early childhood memories. As an impressionable child observing your parents and those around you, you formed your concept of masculinity and femininity. It is important to understand what ideas were implanted then and what events shaped your beliefs later.

Put a check next to each item that was/is true of your father's general view of men and women. Think about your father memories as you work through the list.

My father's general view	of men	of women
Artistic	☐	☐
Capable	☐	☐
Care givers	☐	☐
Creative	☐	☐
Emotional	☐	☐
Faithful	☐	☐
Gentle	☐	☐
Intelligent	☐	☐
Leaders	☐	☐
Logical	☐	☐
Mechanical	☐	☐
Musical	☐	☐
Nurturing	☐	☐
Submissive	☐	☐
Vulnerable	☐	☐
Worthy of respect	☐	☐

As you look over your answers what comes to mind? _____

_____

_____

_____

What do your answers reveal about your father's view of gender roles? _____

_____

_____

Some people hold very rigid role expectations while others are more flexible. Did your dad make exceptions for specific individuals? _____

If you grew up with a sibling of the opposite sex, in what ways did your father treat you alike?

_____

_____

_____

Differently? _____

_____

_____

How has this impacted your view of the opposite sex? _____

_____

_____

Do you agree with your dad about the role of men and women? ☐ Yes ☐ In some areas ☐ No

Explain your answer: _____

_____

Do you think God agrees with your dad about the role of men and women? ☐ Yes ☐ In some areas ☐ No

Explain your answer: _____

_____

Can you think of Bible passages to support your conclusions? _____

_____

A look in the mirror

A person's life is a mirror of his or her priorities and beliefs. People often say they believe something, but their actions do not bear out their beliefs. Just as a look in the mirror can help us make improvements in our appearance, a look at our behavior can help us recognize the need for change.

Do your actions reflect your true beliefs about the roles of men and women? Are your actions in line with God's guidelines?

For Men

Men on television and in movies, especially fathers, are often portrayed as being either incompetent, indecisive clowns or controlling, distant, macho brutes. If either or both of these is any "reflection of society," the current sad state of affairs in the American family should be no surprise.

In his book *Point Man,* Steve Farrar sums up well the task of fathering sons: "It is my God-appointed task to ensure that my sons will be ready to lead a family. I must equip them to that end. Little boys are the hope of the next generation. They are the fathers of tomorrow. They must know who they are and what they are to do. They must see their role model in action. That's how they will know what it means to be a male."[1]

Did your father teach you what it means to be a man? ☐ Yes ☐ No

In what ways? _____

_____

_____

_____

Take a few minutes to compare and contrast what God the Father has to say about manhood and what your dad modeled by answering the following questions.

1. The Bible says that a wise person is open to rebuke and honest confrontation.[2] What did your father teach you or model concerning taking responsibility for your own actions?

_____

_____

_____

2. The Bible says, "A man of knowledge uses words with restraint, and a man of understanding is even-tempered."[3] To experience emotional highs and lows is to be human; to control your responses to these extremes is to be wise. To be *even-tempered* means to be in control of your anger. It doesn't mean you have to be a Milquetoast or an unresponsive iron man. Where did your dad fall on this even-tempered scale? Where do you fall?

1	2	3	4	5	6	7	8	9	10
No expression of anger			Even-tempered		Inappropriate expression of anger				

What effect has this had on your relationships and career? _____

_____

_____

_____

_____

3. The Bible says that a wise man lives for more than money and refuses to let work rule his life.[4] People are more important than things. What was the balance between work and relationships in your dad's life? _____

_____

_____

In your own life? _____

_____

_____

In what ways has the desire to get ahead in the world gotten in the way of your relationships?

_____

_____

4. The Bible says that a wise man takes care of his body and watches what he puts into it.[5] On a scale of 1 to 10—with 1 being poor, 5 average, and 10 excellent—rate your father and yourself in each of the following areas:

	Your father (1-10)	You (1-10)
Exercise	_____	_____
Alcohol consumption	_____	_____
Drug dependency	_____	_____
Rest	_____	_____
Body weight	_____	_____
Healthy eating habits	_____	_____
Caffeine consumption	_____	_____

5. The Bible says that a wise man knows "the condition of his flocks."[6] Leadership is the underpinning of this passage. In today's terms a man's flocks would be his business, his house, his cars, his investments, his total production capacity. We would like to expand this to include the emotional, spiritual, and physical status of his family. In what ways did your dad keep in touch with the condition of his "flock"?

_____

_____

_____

_____

_____

What kind of a leader was your father in:

The workplace? _____

_____

The home? _____

_____

The church or community? _____

_____

What kind of a leader are you in:

The workplace? _____

_____

The home? _____

_____

The church or community? _____

_____

6. The Bible says that a man should "leave his father and mother and be united with his wife."[7] What did your dad model for you in the area of "leaving and cleaving" in marriage?

_____

_____

_____

Do you feel you left your father and your father's control over you and entered into marriage as your own man? ☐ Yes ☐ No

In what ways? _____

_____

_____

For Women

Fathers exert tremendous influence over their daughters' view of themselves and femininity. To a large degree, a little girl will interpret how men, husbands, and fathers are supposed to act based upon what she sees Dad do. And since children are wonderful tape recorders but terrible interpreters, the little girl often makes wrong decisions and inaccurate assumptions about herself and men.

Think about some of the messages your father modeled for you concerning your role as a woman and your view of your femininity. Women have many different roles. Fill in each of the following blanks even if it is not currently one of your roles.

My role as a wife is to: _____

_____

My role as a lover is to: _____

_____

My role as a mother is to: _____

_____

My role as an employee is to: _____

_____

My role as a Christian is to: _____

_____

My role as a woman's friend is to: _____

_____

My role as a man's friend is to: _____

_____

My role caring for myself is to: _____

_____

Proper self-care is sometimes a problem for women. The Bible says that a wise person takes care of his body and watches what he or she puts into it.[8] On a scale from 1 to 10—with 1 being poor, 5 average, and 10 excellent—rate your father and yourself in each of the following areas.

	Your father (1-10)	You (1-10)
Exercise	_____	_____
Alcohol consumption	_____	_____
Drug dependency	_____	_____
Rest	_____	_____
Body weight	_____	_____
Healthy eating habits	_____	_____
Caffeine consumption	_____	_____

In light of the above list, I think I could improve _____

by _____

_____

Roles are an important and necessary part of life. Whereas men and women are equal before God, their roles vary greatly. In marriage, for example, becoming *one* does not mean that a husband and wife are to give up their uniqueness as a man or woman. Role assignments within marriage, such as who balances the check book or feeds the dog, are different for each couple depending on their unique preferences, personalities, and abilities. Each role is needed.

Your father had an impact on your role expectations for your husband. If Dad was mechanical, for example, and Hubby is a klutz with tools, it can create friction.

Think about your father memories and complete the following lists:

Things my father did well	Things my father did poorly
_____	_____
_____	_____
_____	_____
_____	_____
_____	_____

Can you see ways your father's personal strengths and weaknesses have shaped your expectations for your husband? ☐ Yes ☐ No

In what ways? _____

_____

_____

In what ways did your dad shape your expectations for yourself? _____

_____

_____

_____

Think about your father memories as you consider each statement. Put a check next to each dictum that is true of your father's view of women, then comment on how that view has impacted your view of yourself today.

☐ Women are the weaker sex. Impact: _____

_____

☐ Woman are capable. Impact: _____

_____

☐ Woman are to be pretty. Impact: _____

_____

☐ Woman are to be treasured. Impact: _____

_____

☐ Woman are followers. Impact: _____

_____

☐ Woman stay home and raise the children. (☐ Women work outside the home.) Impact:

_____

☐ Woman take care of men. (☐ Men take care of women.) Impact: _____

_____

There is a great deal of confusion today about what our Father in heaven expects of women in general. Such bewilderment can be minimized by thinking in *specific,* rather than *universal,* terms. Thus, the question is, *Which woman are we talking about?* God always deals with us as individuals, not as stereotypes. God's will is not the same for every woman. Women are found in various roles throughout the Bible, and factors such as age, marital status, raising young children, spiritual gifts, and economic status have a bearing on the lifestyle and activities of women in the Bible—and today.

God does, however, give guidelines to help women know what pleases him. For example, Proverbs 31:10-31 talks about a wife of noble character, and Ephesians 5:21-33 discusses the roles of husband and wife.

Read these two passages carefully and jot down your observations.

_____

_____

_____

_____

_____

_____

Titus 2:3-5 gives this counsel: "Teach the older women to be reverent in the way they live, not to be slanderers or addicted to much wine, but to teach what is good. Then they can train the younger women to love their husbands and children, to be self-controlled and pure, to be busy at home, to be kind, and to be subject to their husbands, so that no one will malign the word of God." Most of these guidelines hold true equally for men and women—men should love their wives and children, be self-controlled, kind, not addicted to wine, and so on.

Which instructions apply to your present situation in life? _____

_____

_____

What was hard for you in this section? What was confusing? _____

_____

_____

_____

Authority Figures and Safe Leadership

To a child, nearly everyone around is an authority figure. Toddlers in a crowd can feel lost in a sea of kneecaps. Everything to sustain life and happiness comes from big people who have the power to give and take as they wish. Sadly, many children are raised by "takers." These parents take away their children's sense of self-esteem, value, and dignity.

Some of the ways parents diminish the emotional and physical health of a child are listed below. Because there are no perfect fathers or mothers, each child may feel mistreated in some of these areas. Therefore, try to realistically consider the degree and frequency of each inappropriate behavior in your father memories, rather than adopting an all-or-nothing outlook.

Check each statement that is true of your father.

Giving	*Taking*
☐ Dad encouraged me.	☐ Dad was critical of much I did.
☐ Dad was physically affectionate and gentle.	☐ Dad abused me physically.
☐ Dad exercised self-control.	☐ Dad yelled at me.
☐ Dad respected my privacy.	☐ Dad didn't give me privacy.
☐ Dad tried to understand my concerns.	☐ Dad didn't listen to me.
☐ Dad gave me attention.	☐ Dad didn't spend time with me.
☐ Dad taught me healthy sexuality.	☐ Dad sexually abused me.
☐ Dad respected my opinions.	☐ Dad didn't care what I thought.
☐ Dad was consistent with discipline.	☐ Dad was inconsistent with discipline.
☐ Dad let me enjoy being a kid.	☐ Dad made me grow up too fast.

Each check in the column on the right represents something that was taken from you as a child. In the process you made decisions and assumptions about those in authority over you that led to one of two conclusions:

- Men in authority are only concerned about their agenda, not my feelings.
- Men in authority have my best interest and the good of the group in mind.

As a result, you will tend to project those views onto other authority figures (for example, your boss, supervisor, coach, pastor, policemen, government leaders) in adult life. A teenager who rebelled because Dad never listened may also project those feelings into an employment situation and criticize his boss—but always behind the boss's back because the teenager "knows" that the boss wouldn't listen anyway. In the same way, you can project feelings of confidence and trust in authority into new situations and therefore be willing to give leaders the benefit of the doubt.

When you are confronted by an authority figure, how do you respond? _____

_____

_____

Are there any conclusions you jump to (negative, such as *I'm in trouble now,* or, positive, *My supervisor must have noticed my good work*)? _____

_____

_____

How does your emotional reaction to authority figures relate to the way you responded to your father's authority? _____

_____

Greg was afraid of his father's anger as a child and would run away and hide after he had done something wrong. In college, late one Friday night, Greg sideswiped a parked car. He got scared. His first impulse was to flee the scene before the police could catch him, which he did. The emotional groove of habitual response from childhood overruled his good judgment. As a Christian, Greg was troubled that his automatic impulse was wrong. So after leaving the accident unreported, he even dodged God and was reluctant to pray because he felt God would be mad and eager to punish him.

We can, of course, also be conditioned to respond in inappropriate ways. In what circumstances, if any, do you find yourself reacting to authority like you did when you were a child?

_____

_____

_____

Greg had to realign his thinking with the truth. First, God already knew what he had done, so there was no purpose in not confessing it. Second, God does not punish in unreasonable fits of anger, and God is able to administer discipline whether we are praying or not, so it made no sense for Greg to avoid having a clear conscience and guidance in setting things straight. Third, God says we are to treat others as we want them to treat us, and Greg knew he needed to go back and pay for the damages on the parked car he hit. We wish we could say that Greg did the wise thing by asking God's forgiveness and reporting the accident, but he did not. As a result, although the past is in the past, it still poisons his relationship with God, makes him fearful of being found out, and causes him to think less of himself.

Can you think of times in the past when your first reaction was wrong and you still feel bad about what happened? ☐ Yes ☐ No

If so, what incidents (especially in your father memories) still bother you? _____

_____

_____

_____

_____

_____

If you listed past events above, we encourage you to humbly go to your loving heavenly Father and tell Him you're sorry, then make restoration or apologize to the people involved as God directs. God promises to cleanse our guilty conscience and forgive us: "If we confess our sins, he is faithful and just and will forgive us our sins and purify us from all unrighteousness."[1] God is always willing to restore a relationship with His children. How does that make you feel? _____

_____

If you have difficulty feeling that God likes you and forgives you, remember that feelings lie but God never lies. Jeremiah 17:9 says, "The heart is deceitful." Can you think of times your heart, or emotions, has led you astray? Write down a few instances: _____

_____

_____

_____

Feeling Safe

A child who feels free from rejection, risk, danger, harm, or injury when he or she approaches Dad generally becomes an adult who feels comfortable coming to God or interacting with other authority figures. Feeling safe or unsafe has a great deal to do with how you respond to authority. As a child we each discovered the "safest" way to respond in given situations. And those deeply ingrained patterns seem to continue into adulthood.

What made you feel safe as a child? _____

_____

_____

_____

Was there a certain place you went to for safety? ☐ Yes ☐ No
If so, where _____

_____

Do you have a "safe place" you retreat to now? _____

_____

How did you feel and react as a child when you felt threatened or unsafe emotionally or physically? _____

_____

_____

_____

Has that reaction changed now that you have the power of adulthood? ☐ Yes ☐ No

Explain your answer: _____

_____

_____

When it comes to parenting, too much of a good thing is not a good thing. Overindulgence equals rejection. Did your dad ever do too much for you?

Where the parents do too much for the children, the children will not do much for themselves.

Elbert Hubbard

Safety and Delayed Gratification

M. Scott Peck commented in his national best-seller *The Road Less Traveled,*

As a result of consistent parental love and caring throughout childhood, such fortunate children will enter adulthood not only with a deep internal sense of their own value but also with a deep internal sense of security. . . . With this internal sense of the consistent safety of the world, such a child is *free to delay gratification of one kind or another,* secure in the knowledge that the opportunity for gratification, like home and parents, is always there, available when needed?

The ability to delay gratification is an essential skill for maturity. The inability to delay the gratification of desires is a destructive and common defect in the approach to problem solving.

How would you rate your own willingness to wait? _____

_____

Would you consider yourself to be like your father in this regard? ☐ Yes ☐ No

Explain your answer: _____

_____

_____

The following checklist indicates possible weak areas that can stem from a lack of childhood financial, physical, or emotional security. Check the statements that are true of you.

☐ I purchase items on credit rather than waiting for cash.
☐ I rapidly spend the money I make on immediate needs.
☐ I tend to do things that appear urgent but are not important over time.
☐ I had sex before marriage.
☐ I drank alcohol before being of legal age.
☐ I drove an automobile before having a driver's license.
☐ I snack the minute I feel the urge rather than eating regular meals.
☐ I have rushed ahead of God without waiting for guidance.
☐ I tend to ignore problems rather than putting aside my agenda to deal with them.

Bad habits can stem from an inner ache or feeling that we don't measure up. These feelings may have roots in our father memories, and breaking away from them may not result in the affirmation we hoped to receive from Dad. Try to improve your life because it is what *you* want to do, not because you hope to please your father. This quip from Steven Pearl points out the "I can't win" position some adult children are in.

I phoned my dad to tell him I had stopped smoking. He called me a quitter.

The willingness to wait without impatience is often a good gauge of emotional immaturity or maturity. The first step to curbing a destructive desire for immediate gratification is to recognize that we have a significant problem. The second step is to design an alternative plan of action that will train ourselves to act maturely. For example, if impulse clothes buying is a problem for me, I might set these ground rules. First, I will make a list of things I need to complete my wardrobe at the start of each season *before* I enter a shopping center. Second, I will confine my purchases to items on the list. Third, I will not lead myself into temptation by browsing through attractive catalogues or store displays.

In what area is it hardest for you to wait? _____

Why? _____
_____
_____

What steps could you take to train yourself to respond more maturely in this area?

✔ _____

✔ _____

✔ _____

✔ _____

✔ _____

List the benefits of attaining more self-control in this area:

✔ _____

✔ _____

✔ _____

✔ _____

✔ _____

Learning from the Past

Self-awareness and understanding will do little to change your life if it is not matched with a willingness to learn from the past. After difficulties or successes a wise person questions: What did I do that was worth repeating and worked well? What could I have done differently that would have eased the problems? What, if anything, did I do wrong, and what set me up for those problems?

Joyce's father memories were of a father who drank too much, offered little guidance, squandered the family income, and disciplined unfairly and with no consistency. Here are hard lessons she learned that have greatly improved her adult life:

- Do not date or marry an alcoholic.
- Responsible parenting requires responsible discipline.
- A budget can save a family from financial ruin.
- Love is more than a feeling.
- Criticism hurts people; encouragement builds them up.

Because Joyce was determined not to put herself back into an abusive situation, she refused to date anyone who was not a committed Christian with a history of responsible, kind, self-controlled behavior. It paid off; today she is happily married because she actively decided to break the cycle. Before you move on in this book, take time in prayerful reflection.

What lessons and patterns stand out to you in your father memories and the material we covered? List both positive and painful lessons you can learn from your past.

Lessons to be learned from my past:

✔ _____

✔ _____

✔ _____

✔ _____

✔ _____

✔ _____

✔ _____

↝ _____

↝ _____

↝ _____

Ways I will be better equipped for my future because of past experience:

↝ _____

↝ _____

↝ _____

↝ _____

↝ _____

↝ _____

↝ _____

↝ _____

↝ _____

↝ _____

If you have trouble filling in your list, invite the help of a trustworthy counselor or friend. Share some father memories with him and tell how you felt about what happened. Then ask him how he thinks the past has affected you. Spend some time together looking for past mistakes you continue to repeat, positive behaviors that have become good habits in your life, and other experiences that have helped you to mature.

Start to Keep a Daily Journal

You do not need to be caught unaware by the self-defeating behaviors that keep you from becoming all God created you to be. Stop and think about the ways you relate to people and problems for a few minutes each morning or evening. For example, write out times when you needed to be in control but felt like you lost control. Explain why. Follow up with an entry discussing other ways you could have handled or prevented the situation. List any Bible verses that speak to the issue and prayerfully rehearse in your mind the way you want to do things next time.

Keep the journal simple and enjoyable. The daily exercise of writing in your spiritual journal can greatly increase your progress toward change.

Part Three

TRUTH TO SET YOU FREE

Seeing God in the Image of Our Dad

Because we find it easier to relate to the tangible rather than to the intangible, and to the seen rather than the unseen, our emotional attachment and perception of our earthly fathers shapes our understanding of God. This is not distracting or inappropriate if Dad is a good man and we allow his example to assist us in focusing our adoration of the Lord. But even the best of fathers falls short of the glory of God.

Many of us have heard verses that list attributes of God, such as Nehemiah 9:17: "You are a forgiving God, gracious and compassionate, slow to anger and abounding in love." Even though we may have read what God is like, many of us have never stopped to really think about how God treats people or expresses His love to each of us.

At the core of Christianity are commands to love God with all our hearts, and to love others and ourselves as He has loved us. Understanding God's love for us is the key to understanding how we should treat ourselves, our dad, and others—following the example God set.

Jesus is the only accurate human representation of what God the Father is like. Because we can relate to tangible, flesh-and-blood fathers more easily than to a spiritual being, we tend to bend our perception of God to fit our experience. In Randy's work with father memories, he has repeatedly discovered this pattern:

Those individuals with warm and secure father memories picture God as a warm and secure Father; those with distant or rejecting father memories picture God as distant and rejecting.

As the little child perceives and worships his daddy, the adult perceives and worships his God. Now that we are adults, of course, we have the ability to correct the distortions in our childhood lenses and can learn to see God for who He really is.

What one word represents the image of your earthly father? _____

How does that word fit in with your image of God? _____

_____

_____

_____

Consider your own relationship to your Father in heaven and how it might have been influenced by one of your parents (see *Father Memories*, pages 90-94). Do you see God in the same light as you see your dominant parent or care giver? The doctors at the Minirth-Meier clinic suggest the following exercise.[1]

Check the statements below that reflect your perception of God, then substitute the name of a parent (or someone who raised you) in place of God's name.

☐ 1. "I see God as someone who cares personally and intimately for me and my welfare."

"I see _____ as someone who cares personally and intimately for me and my welfare."

☐ 2. "I view God as a source of nonjudgmental and unconditional love."

"I view _____ as a source of nonjudgmental and unconditional love."

☐ 3. "God is someone with whom I can talk openly and freely about my problems and my needs."

"_____ is someone with whom I can talk openly and freely about my problems and my needs."

☐ 4. "I trust that God hears and responds to my deepest needs and concerns."

"I trust that _____ hears and responds to my deepest needs and concerns."

☐ 5. "I question whether or not God genuinely loves me and accepts me."

"I question whether _____ genuinely loves me and accepts me."

☐ 6. "I see God as a harsh, stern disciplinarian, and I fear His punishment and wrath."

"I see _____ as a harsh, stern disciplinarian, and I fear _____'s punishment and wrath."

☐ 7. "I am angry and bitter at God about past failures or illnesses or disappointments. I wonder why God has not spared me from these."

"I am angry and bitter at _____ about past failures or illnesses or disappointments. I wonder why _____ has not spared me from these."

☐ 8. "God seems distant and remote from me."

"_____ seems distant and remote from me."

☐ 9. "I imagine God's agenda is filled with people and things far more important than I. Surely He doesn't notice me."

"I imagine _____'s agenda is filled with people and things far more important than I. Surely _____ doesn't notice me.

☐ 10. "Some part of me feels so unworthy, I question if I could ever win God's love and approval."

"Some part of me feels so unworthy, I question if I could ever win _____'s love and approval."

God Transcends Father

We serve the Almighty God who draws us to Himself and has supreme power to transcend the influence of our earthly fathers. We do not need to feel afraid or rejected.

> We should not be like cringing, fearful slaves, but we should behave like God's very own children, adopted into the bosom of his family, and calling to him, "Father, Father." For his Holy Spirit speaks to us deep in our hearts and tells us that we really are God's children. And since we are his children, we will share his treasures—for all God gives to his Son Jesus is now ours too.[2]

Yes, God invites us to call Him "Daddy," and we have encouraged you to think about your devotion in this light. But Father is not all that God is. Worship demands that we humbly admit that the reality of the one true God is far beyond our feeble understanding.

Worship requires that we respond to God on a higher level than "father who meets my needs." He is God Most High, infinitely pure love, truth, and power. To Him belong all glory, honor, and praise. Worship takes the focus off our whiney little selves, full of imperfections, flaws, excuses, and hurts, and places the focus on God. God's love can mend broken hearts and heal any hurts from our past. It is great hope and comfort to know:

> *God is bigger than my problems; God is bigger than my pain.*
> *God is beyond what I could hope or think; God is greater than my dreams.*

Attributes of the True God

Even the best of fathers fall far short when compared to a perfect God. When we shrink our image of God to fit the father we see in our memories, we end up with a false god. We tend to expect too much perfection from our earthly fathers and trust too little in the perfection of our heavenly Father.

We've listed a few dominant attributes of the living God. As you compare and contrast your views of Dad and God, think about your level of disappointment when either God or Dad failed to measure up to your expectations.

God is love: "For God so loved . . . that he gave."[3]

In what ways was your father a loving and giving person? _____

_____

_____

What is the most loving thing God ever did for you? _____

_____

At an emotional level, tell how that made you feel (explain with a feeling, not a thought).

_____

_____

_____

God is patient: "The Lord is not slow in keeping his promise, as some understand slowness. He is patient with you, not wanting anyone to perish, but everyone to come to repentance."[4]

In what ways was your father patient or impatient with you? _____

_____

_____

How did you know when your dad ran out of patience? _____

_____

How did you feel and react? _____

_____

Do you ever imagine God's impatience when you repeat a past wrong or fail to follow His instructions? Explain: _____

_____

_____

This imagined impatience or harsh reply from God can easily create distance in your relationship and alter your prayer life. To remind yourself of God's true nature and correct the distorted perceptions you may have, memorize part of Nehemiah 9:17 (which is written below) or another verse that is meaningful to you.

God is forgiving: Nehemiah 9:17 says, "You are a forgiving God, gracious and compassionate, slow to anger and abounding in love."

Did your dad make you feel forgiven, or do you remember feeling like he was always upset over things you did wrong? _____

_____

_____

Lack of forgiveness is often associated with feelings of shame and rejection. This includes self-rejection. Words alone do not make a person "feel" forgiven. The words need to be spoken, but it also takes action. When Christ died on the cross He became a forgiver in action as well as in word. How did you know when your father had really forgiven you for a grievance and your relationship was restored? _____

_____

_____

_____

How do you know when you have forgiven someone who wrongs you? _____

_____

_____

_____

Forgiveness does not mean that what happened was not important or that the person you forgive is not accountable to God for his actions. Is there any person in your past or present whom you have not forgiven? ☐ Yes ☐ No

Who is it hardest for you to forgive? _____

Why? _____

_____

_____

Have you tried to forgive him or her? (If so, what happened; if not, why not?) _____

_____

_____

_____

How would your life be different if you could finally forgive? _____

_____

_____

_____

Forgiveness requires two things: a willing heart and a willing act. In some cases, especially with our own children, it is good to go to them in private and say, "I forgive you." In other cases, it would be unwise or impossible to confront the offender or express your willingness to forgive. But forgiveness is really a matter of your heart response to them, not a means to manipulate a certain response from the one who wronged you.

Think of a person who has been, or is, difficult to forgive. Put his or her name in the blanks below, then complete the sentence. Circle the word in parentheses that best describes your answer.

I (do / don't) bring up the past with _____.

When I think of _____ I (do / don't) feel angry or hurt.

I (do / don't) try to avoid seeing _____. (In some cases avoidance is the best and safest option.)

I am (able /unable) to pray for _____.

I wish the (best /worst) for _____. (It is not necessarily a sign of unforgiveness to long for justice or for God to discipline a wrongdoer. The problem comes when we want to take revenge or see something hurtful happen to even the score.)

I (do / don't) trust God to hold _____ accountable for his or her actions and to bring fair consequences for _____'s actions.

God is fair, faithful, and consistent: "I the Lord do not change."[5]

In what ways is God fair? _____

_____

_____

_____

In what ways is God faithful? _____

_____

_____

_____

In what ways is God consistent? _____

_____

_____

_____

Where would you rate yourself on a consistency/inconsistency scale in each of the following areas:

	Consistent									Inconsistent
Self-discipline	1	2	3	4	5	6	7	8	9	10
Disciplining children	1	2	3	4	5	6	7	8	9	10
Healthy eating habits	1	2	3	4	5	6	7	8	9	10
Finishing what you begin	1	2	3	4	5	6	7	8	9	10
Spending time in prayer	1	2	3	4	5	6	7	8	9	10
Controlling your anger	1	2	3	4	5	6	7	8	9	10
Speaking only the truth	1	2	3	4	5	6	7	8	9	10

There are many wonderful attributes of God. God is perfect love, kindness, truth, and goodness. When our hearts long for perfect closeness and intimacy, we are longing for God. But any person will, at some point or other, let us down. We will let ourselves down. It is important to understand that our goal is not perfection. Our goal is to *make progress* toward becoming more like Christ. As children of God, created in His image, we want our character to take after our Father. We want others to see God in us.

The following list contains several more aspects of God's character that are to be reflected in us. Next to each attribute, write out how your father did in that area and how well you match the description.

God is just: "God 'will give to each person according to what he has done.' "[6]

My father _____

_____

_____

I am _____

_____

_____

God is merciful: "God . . . is rich in mercy."[7] "Who is a God like you. . . . You do not stay angry forever but delight to show mercy."[8]

My father _____

_____

_____

I am _____

_____

_____

God is compassionate: "Because of the Lord's great love we are not consumed, for his compassions never fail. They are new every morning; great is your faithfulness."[9]

My father _____

_____

_____

I am _____

_____

_____

God is holy: "Consecrate yourselves therefore, and be holy; for I am holy."[10]

My father _____

_____

_____

I am _____

_____

_____

God is good: "Good and upright is the Lord; therefore he instructs sinners in his ways."[11]

My father _____

_____

_____

I am _____

_____

_____

God is a protector: "The Lord is good, a refuge in times of trouble. He cares for those who trust in Him."[12]

My father _____

_____

_____

I am _____

_____

_____

God is truthful: "God is not a man, that he should lie."[13] "It is impossible for God to lie."[14] "Jesus answered, 'I am the way and the truth and the life.' "[15]

My father _____

_____

_____

I am _____

_____

_____

We will never measure up to God. And you cannot expect that you or your dad will ever reach that standard. On the other hand, God Himself lives in us to help us grow more like Him. You and I can live in our Father's image.

To crystalize a description of the character God desires you to demonstrate, we are going to look at a familiar passage in 1 Corinthians 13:4-7.

> Love is patient, love is kind. It does not envy, it does not boast, it is not proud. It is not rude, it is not self-seeking, it is not easily angered, it keeps no record of wrongs. Love does not delight in evil but rejoices with the truth. It always protects, always trusts, always hopes, always perseveres.

Because God is love, we encourage you to read through this passage aloud, putting "God" in the blank provided. Then, go back and write your name in each of the blanks and read it again. This can be considered a mission statement for a child of God who wants to be like his or her Father in heaven.

_____ is patient, _____ is kind. _____ does not envy,

_____ does not boast, _____ is not proud. _____ is not

rude, _____ is not self-seeking, _____ is not easily angered,

_____ keeps no record of wrongs. _____ does not delight in evil

but rejoices with the truth. _____ always protects, always trusts, always hopes, always perseveres.

Beginning Here and Now

Steve said he greatly benefited from one of his grandfather's tidbits of wisdom. One afternoon Steve was complaining about his life, and Grandfather remarked simply, "Wherever you are is where you are. And you can't change the facts."

There are certain "givens" in the equation of life. No matter how much you may wish you had been born into another family or been blessed with more abilities or arrived at a different position in life . . .

✓ You are who you are.
✓ You are where you are.
✓ You can't change the facts.

We need to be willing to move forward in life by making use of the strengths and resources we have available at this particular moment. Think about all the good things that you have to work with and complete the following lists.

The ten best things that are true about me as a person:

1. _____
2. _____
3. _____
4. _____
5. _____
6. _____
7. _____
8. _____
9. _____
10. _____

The ten best things that are true about my childhood:

1. _____
2. _____
3. _____
4. _____
5. _____
6. _____
7. _____
8. _____
9. _____
10. _____

The ten best things that are true about my life now:

1. _____
2. _____
3. _____
4. _____
5. _____
6. _____
7. _____
8. _____
9. _____
10. _____

Satan tries to convince us that we don't have the wisdom or the ability to be the person God wants us to be. The lie is that we don't have the tools to build a good life or to do God's will—so we can't be held responsible. But the truth is that God has given us the Holy Spirit and the Bible for instruction so that "the man [or woman] of God may be adequate, equipped for every good work."[16]

Taking Responsibility for Yourself

Whatever your childhood was, it is over now. It is helpful to understand the dynamics at work in your response to life, but ultimately the only one who can make any changes is you. Don't wait for your father to somehow set everything straight. And don't wait for God, like a great fairy godmother, to wave a magic wand and give you a Cinderella story. It is remarkable what we can do with ourselves if we try.

Let your dignity return. Stop making excuses. See yourself as a contributing adult, not as some poor thing who was mistreated and can never get over it. *Self-pity is the enemy of maturity.*

By contrast, developing a balanced sense of responsibility is a key to self-discipline and emotional control. Maturity means avoiding the two destructive extremes. Noted psychiatrist M. Scott Peck explains:

> Most people who come to see a psychiatrist are suffering from what is called either a neurosis or a character disorder. Put most simply, these two conditions are disorders of responsibility, and as such they are opposite styles of relating to the world and its problems. The neurotic assumes too much responsibility; the person with a character disorder not enough. When neurotics are in conflict with the world they automatically assume that they are at fault. When those with character disorders are in conflict with the world they automatically assume that the world [or someone else in it] is at fault.[1]

Consider which side of the responsibility scale you most easily slide to when things get out of balance. Check the statements that apply:

I tend to assume too much responsibility.

- ☐ When something goes wrong I don't feel at ease—I must be doing something wrong.
- ☐ I tell myself often that I ought to do this or I should be able to do that.
- ☐ I often think: If I would only do _____, then the problem would be solved.
- ☐ I feel bad for anyone who faces something unpleasant and want to step in to fix it.
- ☐ It's all up to me; you get out of life just what you put into it.
- ☐ I feel I always fall short of the mark; I can't seem to measure up.
- ☐ I am guilt ridden about my behavior as a spouse, parent, employee, or Christian.
- ☐ I messed up my parents' lives.

I tend to assume too little responsibility.

- ☐ People can make me mad or upset me.
- ☐ I tend to avoid or escape responsibility for my own actions.
- ☐ I like to be led and figure that, if someone else told me to do it, then it's not my fault what happened.

☐ When confronted about a problem I often deny it or blame others.
☐ When my children or employees have difficulty, I lay the blame on the "system" (the schools, racism, sexism, governmental policy, peer pressure, and so on).
☐ I often excuse my conduct by saying I'm sick or fatigued or overstressed.
☐ Others are responsible to meet my needs and assist me in reaching my goals.
☐ My parents messed up my life.

You are not responsible for the rain that falls, but only for your reaction to it.
Virginia Satir

The leaning toward either extreme in our sense of responsibility makes us ineffective and destructive in our friendships, home life, business dealings, and spiritual life. Even in our devotional life we may teeter-totter over the "God's part/my part" balance. And like men and women through the ages, we find our hearts echoing the classic Serenity Prayer:

God grant me the serenity to accept the things I cannot change, the courage to change the things I can, and the wisdom to know the difference.

We often avoid taking responsibility to change the things that we can improve. Below are listed some common ways to cope with the guilt of irresponsibility. Check the immature coping mechanisms you have used in the past:

☐ Denying the problem
☐ Blaming someone else
☐ Feeling sorry for yourself
☐ Assuming a victim mentality
☐ Projecting your feelings onto others
☐ Making excuses
☐ Positioning yourself to look good or come out on top, regardless of the outcome

I am responsible for how I relate and respond to you, regardless of how you relate and respond to me. For example, my attitude of disrespect or my unwillingness to talk truthfully and directly in our relationship is my problem. I alone am responsible for me; you cannot control my attitude or response. Those are my choices, my responsibility.

List circumstances, feelings, and behaviors you need to take proper responsibility for in your relationship with your father or with God.

✔ _____

✔ _____

✔ _____

✔ _____

✔ _____

✔ _____

✔ _____

On the other hand, we can easily assume too much responsibility for others, which leads to attempts to manipulate, dominate, or control them. List circumstances, relationships, or self-talk where you need to let go or assume less responsibility.

✔ _____

✔ _____

✔ _____

✔ _____

✔ _____

✔ _____

✔ _____

The Decision to Heal

We behave ourselves into trouble; we need to behave ourselves out of it. Talking, thinking, and even praying is not enough. Words of apology often accompany the behavior, but words without action are hollow. The process of mending relationships and making change takes three steps:

1. You sense that something is wrong.
2. You identify the problem.
3. You determine what to do, and take action.

With good counselors there is safety.   Proverbs 11:14, TLB

If you are feeling overwhelmed by your past, we encourage you to seek help from a good counselor. The Bible says it is wise to ask for counsel when making important decisions.

Do you need healing in your relationship with Dad or sense areas that could be improved?
☐ Yes ☐ No

Are you ready for the process to begin? ☐ Yes ☐ Not now (if you know there is a problem but are not prepared to commit to a plan of action as God directs, don't pretend. God knows your heart, and your loved ones will see through your empty words. You will only deceive yourself.)

Step two of the process is to identify the problem. You probably have a handle on the symptoms, but do you really understand the underlying problem? If you are confused about the issues at the core of the problem we suggest that you take time daily to pray specifically for wisdom and seek a clearer understanding. Then ask, What is the real problem here, and how far back does it go?

The real problem is _____

_____

_____

I think it all started when _____

_____

_____

Here are some typical problems that can mess up the father/child relationship. Check those that have created distance or friction between you and your dad.

- ☐ Poor communication
- ☐ Rejection
- ☐ Anger
- ☐ Value differences
- ☐ Lack of appreciation
- ☐ Selfishness
- ☐ Rebellion
- ☐ Abuse
- ☐ Manipulation or control
- ☐ Comparison with others

For each item you checked, explain the impact that problem has had on your relationship in the past and present.

_____

_____

_____

_____

_____

_____

Step three is the big one—*action*. Determine a plan of action, and get with it. Throughout this workbook we have been encouraging you to take one form of action or another. The only way to reach greater maturity and experience healing is to take action. If you have an area needing attention and you have some idea of what to do first then we ask you to consider why you have put things off until now.

I waited until now to deal with this issue because _____

_____

_____

It takes time to take action. Since we cannot change everything at once, it is wise to break your plan of action into small, manageable steps. The following section will help you determine where to begin. Choose one particular area to work on.

In what ways did you, or do you, contribute to the problem? _____

_____

_____

_____

In what ways are you willing to change your thinking and self-talk? _____

_____

_____

_____

In what ways are you willing to change your behavior toward this person or situation?

_____

_____

_____

How would these new behaviors on your part change the situation? _____

_____

_____

_____

How would these behavioral changes improve your life? _____

_____

_____

_____

Christian growth and mending relationships require a process, not an isolated act. It will take time. Be realistic in your self-expectations.

How much time are you willing to give to the process? _____

What benchmarks (change in attitude, change in feelings, change in response, and so on) will you use to determine your progress? _____

_____

_____

_____

Will you set up some way to keep yourself accountable, or give someone else the opportunity to keep you in line with your goals? _____

When will you begin? _____

We suggest you start today.

> *Men stumble over the truth*
> *from time to time*
> *but most pick themselves up*
> *and hurry off*
> *as if nothing happened.*
>
> Sir Winston Churchill

Turning Anger into Action

There is not a lot to be gained from getting frustrated over the shortcomings in our character or the flaws and failures in our past—unless our anger motivates constructive action. As Malcolm X noted, "Usually when people are sad, they don't do anything. They just cry over their condition. But when they get angry, they bring about a change."[2]

List any memories from your past that left you feeling frustrated or angry.

✔ _____

✔ _____

✔ _____

✔ _____

✔ _____

✔ _____

✔ _____

Channeling our anger into constructive outlets is not always easy, but it is possible. Anger over injustice and oppression has been the steel in the backbone of many brave men and women throughout history. Many social changes, such as the abolishment of slavery and exploitive child labor, are the direct result of individuals who got mad enough to effectively and persistently fight the system. Sometimes the "system" you must fight is the system of thought within your own mind—the downward pull of destructive and distorted messages such as "I don't have any choice," "God's children are supposed to suffer," or "You'll never amount to anything."

One young man from a poor family who wanted to become a doctor was insulted and discouraged by his father for his "daydreams and foolish notions." Looking back, the man remarked, "I got so mad when Dad told me it couldn't be done that I promptly shut up and set about to prove him wrong by doing it!"

Sometimes healthy anger prompts us to break the silence and speak out rather than quietly swallowing our hurt. When we speak the truth in love calmly and directly, we can begin to take a proactive part in relationships rather than the passive role of a little child.

Now list constructive ways that anger can fuel your desire to change.

✔ _____

✔ _____

✔ _____

✔ _____

✔ _____

✔ _____

✔ _____

✔ _____

Healthy Closeness and Trust

It's hard to trust someone you are angry with, or someone who is mad at you. To be trusted is a privilege, not a right. If your father memories reveal an attitude of mutual trust, you are very fortunate. Because if your father earned your trust, trusting others today is generally easier. On the other hand, if your father betrayed your trust it may be difficult to get close to others.

Trusting someone means having confidence in that person—confidence that how you act, how you feel, and even what you say will not jeopardize your relationship. You have confidence that he or she will do what he says he will do and will believe the best in you. Our Father in heaven is the ultimate example of a person worthy of trust and forever faithful.

Trust is at the foundation of all healthy relationships. Can you think of someone you find hard to trust because he or she has betrayed a confidence or broken a promise?

_____

Has it ever been difficult for you to trust your father? Explain. _____

_____

_____

Has it ever been difficult to win your father's trust? Explain. _____

_____

_____

_____

List the names of three people you would like to trust more:

- _____
- _____
- _____

Put a check next to each statement that is true concerning your father, spouse (if married), and closest friend. If your father or spouse is deceased or out of your life, then answer the question based on your last memories of that relationship.

Father	Spouse	Friend	
☐	☐	☐	I can express my feelings openly.
☐	☐	☐	I feel safe in their presence.
☐	☐	☐	I feel understood and accepted.
☐	☐	☐	I want their input in my life.
☐	☐	☐	They tell me the truth, even if it hurts.
☐	☐	☐	What I share in private stays between us.
☐	☐	☐	I can believe what they tell me.
☐	☐	☐	I know they will keep their promises.
☐	☐	☐	If I was in trouble, they would be there for me.

In the same way that trust is essential when relating to our loved ones, our relationship with God hinges on trust. The Bible tells us that without faith it is impossible to please God.[3] Do you trust God? ☐ Yes ☐ No

In the following list we will take the questions above and replace your earthly father with God the Father. It will test your feelings about trusting God.

☐ I can express my feelings openly to God in prayer.
☐ I feel safe in God's presence.
☐ I feel understood and accepted by God.
☐ I want God's input in my life.
☐ God will tell me the truth, even if it hurts.
☐ What I share in private prayer stays between us—I feel no need to tell others.
☐ I can believe what God tells me.
☐ I know God will keep His promises.
☐ If I was in trouble, God would be there for me.

Learning and earning trust is a process. Take small steps. Plan to fail occasionally, but keep going. Here are four important steps toward healthy trust.

1. *Know who to trust and who not to trust.*

There are some people who are not worthy of our trust. If someone repeatedly violates our trust we are right to hesitate before making ourselves vulnerable again. List the names of three people you really trust and explain why.

Name _____

Why? _____

_____

Name _____

Why? _____

_____

Name _____

Why? _____

_____

Now list the name of one person you do not trust now, but would like to.

Name _____

Why don't you fully trust him or her? _____

_____

_____

What would he or she need to do for you to develop greater trust? _____

_____

_____

_____

What would you need to change for him or her to trust you more? _____

_____

_____

_____

In some cases your emotional, physical, and spiritual safety is more important than trying to develop trust. If you sense that trusting another person, no matter who it is, would result in being taken advantage of, injured, or hurt, *keep a safe distance in the relationship.* There are no acceptable terms for healthy trust other than the mutual safety, respect, and good of both people involved.

2. *Become a trustworthy person.*

Trust must go both ways. Is there anyone who has difficulty trusting you? (If so, who and why?) _____

_____

_____

_____

In what ways is their lack of trust justified? _____

_____

_____

Do you want to earn back their trust? _____ If so, what would it take to do so?

_____

_____

The following quiz will help you evaluate how worthy of trust you really are. Circle the response that is true of you.

Yes	No	I keep private information someone tells me strictly confidential.
Yes	No	I tell my friends and family the truth in a loving way.
Yes	No	I think the best when I hear a rumor concerning someone I know.
Yes	No	I don't repeat a story without verifying the facts.
Yes	No	I don't use people to achieve selfish purposes.
Yes	No	I refuse to enter into conversations based on hearsay, gossip, or criticism.
Yes	No	I keep my word.
Yes	No	I follow through on my promises.
Yes	No	I never turn on my friends or loved ones.

In what ways did your father contribute to your becoming a trustworthy person? _____

_____

_____

In what ways did your father undermine your trustworthiness (if at all)? _____

_____

_____

3. *Take a small step.*

Relationships are not static. We are either moving toward one another or we are moving apart. Which way are you moving? Think for a moment about that one person you would like to trust more. What small step can you take today to move toward him or her in a safe way? _____

_____

_____

Keep in mind these general safeguards for avoiding potential problems:

- ✔ Never tell young children (or let them overhear) things you don't want repeated.
- ✔ Share personal prayer requests when you plan to pray together personally—not over the phone, in print, or at a public meeting.
- ✔ Talk about personal matters only with one or two most trusted friends.
- ✔ Never tell *anyone* about your sex life, private medical problems, or net worth—some things should stay between husband and wife.
- ✔ Stay away from abusive people; there are plenty of good friends in the world.

4. *Act with the end in mind.*

The pyramid chart below is taken from a book Rita coauthored with Richard Fowler of the Minirth-Meier clinic.[4] Notice that different amounts of sharing and closeness are appropriate for relationships in each of the five general stages.

Pyramid of Interpersonal Relationships

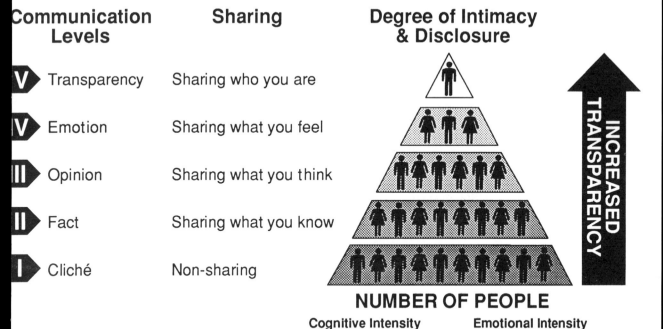

Communication Levels	Sharing	Degree of Intimacy & Disclosure
V Transparency	Sharing who you are	
IV Emotion	Sharing what you feel	
III Opinion	Sharing what you think	
II Fact	Sharing what you know	
I Cliché	Non-sharing	

NUMBER OF PEOPLE

Cognitive Intensity   Emotional Intensity

INCREASED TRANSPARENCY

Determine what level of relationship you desire with a given person, then consider the safe degree of trust and intimacy. The level of closeness I desire with _____ is _____.

I am willing to pursue this level of disclosure and trust by _____

_____

_____

_____

When you act with the end in mind you are less likely to move too far too fast in a relationship or get "burned" by becoming emotionally vulnerable to someone who is not committed to your well-being. With your father, as with anyone else, the better you get to know one another and the more time you have spent together, the greater the degree of trust that generally develops in the relationship.

You Have Choices; You Can Change

If your father is still living, check any of the changes in your relationship that you feel could realistically be made now. For the time being, the list will focus only on those things that can be improved by your attitude or conduct, not those changes your father controls.

☐ I could hug Dad more often.
☐ I could speak more respectfully.
☐ I could communicate my decisions more clearly.
☐ I could pray for him more.
☐ I could spend more time with Dad.
☐ I could grumble and criticize less.
☐ I could avoid pointless discussions when our opinions differ.
☐ I could control the times, locations, and length of our visits.
☐ I could quit talking about him and start talking to him.
☐ I could express my appreciation and thanks more openly.

Choose any one of the items you checked and imagine how it might improve your attitude toward your father. Remember that a constant enemy to strong relationships is the lie *Nothing I do matters anyway, so why bother?* One of the most disabling characteristics of distressed individuals is that their thoughts become so distorted that it appears they have no choices; they are completely trapped. We do, however, always have options. We have choices—even if the choice is simply our heart attitude as we endure circumstances beyond our control.

God has given you authority over you, and what you do makes a great difference in the quality of your life. "For God did not give us a spirit of timidity, but a spirit of power, of love and of self-discipline."[1]

Recovering Your Choices

Each of us was greatly influenced by our childhood—positively or negatively. And at sometime or other we've all heard someone say something like

"That's just the way I am."
"That's the way our family has always done things; I come by it naturally."
"Like father, like son."

When someone makes statements like that, they are really saying that the past programming they received is influencing their behavior. Does that mean they have no choice in the matter? Not at all.

The way you act today is a direct result of the choices you make now. The degree to which you build on, or choose to override, your inner porgramming is entirely up to you. You are the one living your life, and God is willing to guide you toward maturity and healthy, satisfying relationships.

Because you are created in the image of God, you have the ability to think, create, and choose. You can choose to pattern your character and thinking upon God's truth and the example of Christ rather than simply acting out a life-script around your dad's expectations for you. Of course, many of your father's desires for you will be healthy and good. But you still need to exercise your choice to make them your desires and goals.

Check the ways in which you can exercise healthy spiritual initiative:

☐ I will pray.
☐ I will choose moral friends who respect and support me.
☐ I will seek counsel from others before making important decisions.
☐ I will memorize and meditate on what God says in the Bible.
☐ I will make decisions instead of following feelings shaped by past experience.
☐ I will refuse to accept old conditioning that leads me away from my true goals.
☐ I will not put off making minor decisions that set the tone of my everyday life.
☐ I will _____

_____

_____

_____

_____

_____

_____

Affirming Your Desire to Change

Select a single area and make a simple decision to change; then act on it. That is how you gain control of your life and become the person God created you to be—a little at a time, a day at a time. Repeating positive affirmations can help you in the process of change.

These samples of inner dialogue fit the biblical concept of renewing your mind; they are simply an aid to train and discipline your thought life. There is nothing hypnotic, mystic, or subliminal about these statements. Rather, they are simply positive affirmations that lead to spiritual, emotional, and social growth.

Check an affirmation statement that encourages and empowers you to take control of your life, or write one in your own words. The brain responds best to statements in first person, present tense like those below. It may feel more comfortable for you to approach the statements like a prayer, prefacing them with the thought, "Through the power of God at work in me . . ."

☐ "I am capable of changing my behavior and I choose to do so. I choose to be in control of me. And I see encouraging progress each and every day."

☐ "I will not be mastered by anything. I refuse to yield to bad habits or destructive thought patterns in my life. By taking control of my life, minute by minute, day by day, I accomplish lasting change."

☐ "I take the initiative to take control of my life. I submit myself to God—and God is doing a great work in me. Today and tomorrow are exciting for me as I become all God wants me to be."

☐ "I no longer let myself be pushed around by past conditioning, circumstances, or other peoples' expectations. I take the time to consider God's Word and keep myself under His control."

☐ "I enjoy the confidence of making decisions based on biblical convictions regardless of messages from my past. Knowing God supports my decisions gives me the determination to act on them. I always think things through, make a decision, then follow through."

☐ "_____

_____

_____

_____"

Remember that the statements are to affirm your goals and the process of change; don't worry if they are not completely true of you *yet*. Consider them statements of intent, not boastful or proud comments that you have arrived at maturity.

After you have selected an affirmation that especially encourages you, write it in the blanks provided every morning and evening for one week. Pray about your desire to take control of your life. You may find it helpful to continue this practice for several days or to memorize the affirmation and replay it in your memory whenever you feel discouraged.

Daily Affirmations

Day 1   Morning: _____

_____

_____

Evening: _____

_____

_____

Day 2   Morning: _____

_____

_____

Evening: _____

_____

_____

Day 3   Morning: _____

_____

_____

Evening: _____

_____

_____

Day 4   Morning: _____

_____

_____

Evening: _____

_____

_____

Day 5   Morning: _____

_____

Evening: _____

_____

_____

Day 6   Morning: _____

_____

_____

Evening: _____

_____

_____

Day 7   Morning: _____

_____

_____

Evening: _____

_____

_____

Part Four

DEALING WITH YOURSELF, YOUR FATHER, AND OTHERS NOW

Stepping Ahead in Life

We each experience countless hurts, disappointments, and loses throughout life. Some of those painful past experiences no longer affect the way we live or influence our emotions. But the exercises you have completed thus far probably indicated a few hurts that you are hanging on to. If not, you need to seriously consider whether or not you have moved beyond a universal coping mechanism—*denial*.

Moving Beyond Denial

You may be afraid to face the pain of your past, afraid you might drown in your tears—or, worse, conclude that after your best effort the wound cannot be healed. Then you would lose all hope. And as silly as it sounds, most of us would rather cling to the imaginary chance that the problem will somehow go away if we ignore it long enough than deal with reality. You may also fear rejection or misunderstanding from others close to you, or even the despair of confusion within yourself. Denial is often a subconscious mechanism that seeks to protect you from feelings you fear will overwhelm you, destroy you, or keep you from thinking clearly enough to respond in the immediate situation.

If you found yourself ignoring, overlooking, or somehow dismissing certain portions of your past as you completed these exercises, then you are experiencing some degree of denial. In their book *Forgiveness,* Sidney and Suzanne Simon suggest that you may be in a stage of denial if you find yourself thinking that old injuries and injustices are

- unimportant
- water under the bridge
- irrelevant to your life today
- not worth dredging up again
- over and done with
- better off forgotten

By contrast, the Simons suggest that people who are willing to confront the hurts they have been hiding from themselves and move on toward forgiveness and maturity use nondenial statements.[1]

Check those that you remember thinking to yourself or telling someone.

- [ ] "I was hurt."
- [ ] "What happened to me still hurts."
- [ ] "That was no way to treat me."
- [ ] "It was wrong."
- [ ] "I've suffered because of what I went through."
- [ ] "I haven't gotten over it yet."
- [ ] "It *was* that bad."

But . . .

- [ ] "God accepts me just as I am, with the past I can't change."
- [ ] "I can talk about the experience without self-destruction."
- [ ] "I do not have to shut down my feelings or push things to the back of my mind to survive."
- [ ] "I can live with a clean, honest, acceptance of my past."

Getting Past Self-Blame

Many people move out of denial directly into self-blame. Children are especially prone to take a self-centered view of experiences, considering themselves responsible for every bad thing that happens. Dr. Simon explains: "While in the self-blame stage, you decide that bad things happened to you because:

- [ ] you did something to make them happen;
- [ ] you were not good enough in some way;
- [ ] you did not do what you could have done to prevent them from happening;
- [ ] you set yourself up to be hurt by expecting too much or ignoring the signs of impending disaster."[2]

Here again the imbalance is that you hold yourself accountable for other people's actions, absolving them of all responsibility. The problem is one of focus—you focus exclusively on what you did to deserve it or did not do to prevent it. Self-blame hinges on an exaggerated sense of self-importance. Humility is the escape hatch that can free you.

As a humble person you can admit that you are not the center of the universe, you are not capable of perfection, and you acknowledge that the actions of others bring consequences. You are free to forgive yourself and seek forgiveness from your heavenly Father for your wrong actions, and you are free to allow other people to be responsible for their actions also. Consider the following verse: "Humble yourselves, therefore, under the mighty hand of God, that He may exalt you at the proper time, casting all your anxiety upon Him, because He cares for you."[3]

Do you find the idea of humility appealing or disagreeable? Explain _____

_____

_____

_____

Have you ever connected the concept of exaggerated self-blame with pride? ☐ Yes ☐ No

Do you feel there is a valid connection? _____

_____

Either extreme—destructive self-blame or the opposite imbalance of a victim mentality—will damage your present relationships. Do you feel you have good balance in the admission of your role in past and present problems? ☐ Yes ☐ No

How could you make improvements? _____

_____

_____

_____

_____

> *As one goes through life one learns that if you don't paddle your own canoe,*
> *you don't move.*
>
> Katherine Hepburn

Reparenting Yourself

Sidney Simons and his wife Suzanne include an instructive passage on how to treat yourself with respect and compassion:

You must begin to take care of your inner child instead of neglecting or abusing it. You must listen to the part of yourself that tells you that you feel sad, scared, or abandoned and comfort that vulnerable child inside you. How do you do that? Well, how would you comfort a real child who was hurting? To start with, you could listen and pay attention to what he has to say, trying to understand what he was feeling and why. Then you might:

- make motherly, nurturing statements like "It's okay. It will be all right. I'll help you through this."
- give him a little gift
- take him to a place he finds fun, peaceful, or relaxing

- give him time to himself
- let him cry
- let his household chores wait while he takes a nap or goes for a walk or draws a picture
- assure him that he was loved by you and remind him of the qualities that make him a unique, lovable, capable, worthwhile human being
- make sure that he knows that the hurtful thing that happened to him was not "all his fault"

To finally let yourself "off the hook" and stop perpetuating your pain, you must do these very things *for yourself,* right down to allowing yourself to experience the joy, playfulness, and spontaneity that you may have missed during your real childhood.[4]

Everyone must row with the oars he has.   English Proverb

How would you rate your own ability to treat yourself with proper tenderness and encouragement? _____

_____

_____

Go back through the above list and consider which ways you could begin to better take care of yourself. What do you plan to do differently? _____

_____

_____

_____

If you are a parent, consider how you can break the negative cycles from your childhood and accentuate the positive with your own children. What comes to mind as an initial step you would like to take? _____

_____

_____

_____

Are you committed enough to make a change, or are you just thinking about it?_____

_____

_____

_____

> *It is only when you exercise your right to choose that you can also exercise your right to change.*
>
> Dr. Shad Helmstetter[5]

Developing Healthy Habits

By creating new habits of response you can override the ineffective patterns you learned in the past. Without proper habits we flounder; we lack clear direction. We suffer "decision overload" because there is no routine order and structure to fall back on.

List the three habits you feel benefit you most in your life today:

* _____
* _____
* _____

Can you think of any poor habits you would be better off without? List the three habits that you would most like to change.

* _____
* _____
* _____

> Some of us attempt to rule ourselves by shoulds and shouldn'ts. But consider:
> *Laws are never as effective as habits.*
>
> Adlai Stevenson

Put a check where you are today:

Spiritual habits

1	2	3	4	5	6	7	8	9	10
Bad habits				Working at it					Good habits

Health and hygiene habits

1	2	3	4	5	6	7	8	9	10
Bad habits				Working at it					Good habits

Conversation habits

1	2	3	4	5	6	7	8	9	10
Bad habits				Working at it				Good habits	

Problem-solving habits

1	2	3	4	5	6	7	8	9	10
Bad habits				Working at it				Good habits	

Mental habits

1	2	3	4	5	6	7	8	9	10
Bad habits				Working at it				Good habits	

Social habits

1	2	3	4	5	6	7	8	9	10
Bad habits				Working at it				Good habits	

Listening habits

1	2	3	4	5	6	7	8	9	10
Bad habits				Working at it				Good habits	

Now go back through the above inventory and put an X where you would like to be ninety days from now. Often the first step—making the commitment to change—is the most difficult. Once you have made that decision do not give up because of any lapse back into your old ways. Plod along the path toward change. Persistence pays.

If we don't change our direction, we're likely to end up where we're headed.
Chinese Proverb

Take a thorough inventory of who you are and what you have done with your life. What do you want to become? Are you on the right path, or are you plodding on in the wrong direction, numbly ruining your chances of ever satisfying the deepest desires of your heart?

Habits That Get Out of Control

Habits that get out of control are called addictions. Even good behaviors, like working hard or exercising regularly, can become compulsive and drive us toward unhealthy extremes. Are you out of control in any of the following areas?

- ☐ Food
- ☐ Drugs
- ☐ Dependency
- ☐ Security
- ☐ Exercise
- ☐ Speech

- ☐ Money
- ☐ Service
- ☐ Selfishness
- ☐ Relationships
- ☐ Excitement
- ☐ Other: _____

We can also get in the habit of letting our emotions rule the roost. It can be exhilarating to let our emotions go or comforting to bury them inside, but we can quickly find ourselves losing control. Circle your response:

Yes   No   Do emotions dictate many of your decisions in life?

Yes   No   Do you say what you feel like saying instead of controlling your tongue?

Yes   No   Is it difficult for you to keep your emotions in check?

Yes   No   Are you easily bothered or upset by the behavior of others?

Yes   No   Do you use emotional outbursts to control the behavior of others?

Yes   No   Do you "stuff" your emotions inside because you are uncomfortable?

Yes   No   Do you discourage any show of emotion from others?

How do you typically respond to feelings of:

- fear _____
- worry _____
- anger _____
- insecurity _____
- joy _____
- affection _____
- worship _____

In what ways would you like to change your habits of handling emotions? _____
_____
_____
_____

Make a list of what it would take to develop new habits in the areas you listed. _____
_____
_____
_____

Are you willing to do the things on your list—daily? If so, when? _____
_____
_____

If not, why not? _____

_____

_____

Can you think of anyone who models the kind of behavior you would like to learn? ☐ Yes
☐ No

Is so, what can you learn by studying their responses and example? _____

_____

_____

_____

Do you think the individual would be willing to help you? ☐ Yes ☐ No

If so, would you be willing to seek his or her advice? ☐ Yes ☐ No

Explain why or why not. _____

_____

_____

As you leave this section remember these important points:

- We tend to limit God because of the experience and memories we have of our father.
- We underestimate God's care, concern, and love for us, and in the process stifle real fellowship.
- We can never completely experience God the Father for who He is until we forgive our earthly father for what he wasn't.
- We are created in the image of God, and with His help we can become more and more like our Father in heaven.

Dealing with a Difficult Father Today

In *Father Memories* Randy Carlson shared stories from his own childhood. He went on to suggest the following steps to begin the process of putting the past behind you, personalizing each application:

1. *Don't pull away emotionally:* I'm thankful for a wonderful wife and good friends who help me out here.
2. *Flip the coin:* I'm discovering there's another side to my life story, including my father memories.
3. *Uncover the lie:* There is no need to tell myself that I'm stupid or have to please everyone—that's a lie.
4. *Accept the past for what it was:* In my case, it was pretty good, so thank you, Lord.
5. *Learn from your hurts:* In my memories there were lessons to be learned about better ways to handle feelings of embarrassment and rejection.
6. *Don't let your father memories define who you are:* I am more capable than I've told myself for years—and so are you.

In the sections of *Father Memories* that followed, Randy elaborated on each of the above steps. It might be helpful to review that material (begnning on page 174) before continuing. In what ways have you begun to take the steps listed above? _____

_____

_____

_____

Those who desire an ongoing relationship with a difficult father will find the next few pages of material helpful. The exercises are designed to give you practical steps toward an improved relationship.

If your father was abusive, overbearing, or nonsupportive in the past, it is essential for you to set up new ground rules for present and future interactions. First, you will need to structure the physical environment in your favor. For example, limit the visit to a nice dinner together, rather than an entire holiday or weekend. Avoid stressful settings, such as a sibling's home, where inappropriate and hurtful comparisons always come up. And choose times when all family members are rested, involved in directed activity, and surrounded by people who affirm healthy relational patterns. Don't set yourself up in a no-win situation.

Structuring Your Visit

Before scheduling your next meeting with your father, think through the probable consequences of your choices:

When Dad and I meet, do I want anyone else to be present? Why or why not? _____
_____
_____

If so, my backup support people are _____
_____ .

Other family members are most likely to undercut my desire for change if I get together with Dad at _____
_____ .

Why? _____
_____
_____

Other family members are generally supportive and things are most likely to go smoothly if we see each other at _____
_____ .

Therefore, to take care of myself I'm going to _____
_____ .

How long will you choose to be with your father? _____

Limiting the visit can be best accomplished by setting up a specific time frame, hemmed in by deadlines (such as lunch, with a specific time you need to be back at work). What specific things will you do to control the length and setting of the encounter? _____
_____
_____
_____

OK, when will I meet Dad and on what turf? Why have I chosen this time? _____
_____
_____
_____

I will make the length and location of the visit perfectly clear from the first. This is what I want to say and do to set up our meeting: _____
_____
_____

_____

_____

_____

_____

_____

This is what I want to say and do when we're together: _____

_____

_____

_____

_____

_____

_____

Ground Rules for Healthy Conversation

Dealing with a difficult father as an adult will require a constant string of controlled confrontations. When patterns of conversation surface that you now recognize as dysfunctional, you must face up to your father. That is best accomplished by setting ground rules for healthy conversation that you both agree to *before* you begin to talk. These are basic understandings that:

- You agree to hear one another out without interrupting or accusing.
- You will not allow name-calling, yelling, or swearing.
- You will not lie to one another.

What will you say to establish these ground rules? _____

_____

_____

_____

Rehearse your opening remarks until they are direct, clear, and spoken in a nondefensive tone of voice. It may also be helpful to role play the upcoming conversation with a friend in order to feel more comfortable setting up the initial guidelines.

Many adults who were raised in emotionally unhealthy homes are drawn into abusive, unsatisfying, or belittling conversations because they duplicate childhood dynamics. You must refuse to use the old script or accept old labels and roles. The new you, empowered by the Holy Spirit, can learn to converse according to the healthy guidelines above. To do so you must be willing to face up to your father in a firm, controlled way. You will need a strategy for enforcing the rules.

Check any statements on this list that would be helpful as you talk to your father:

☐ "It's not OK for you to talk to me that way. Remember we agreed to . . ."

☐ "This is a good example of the disrespectful way you talk to me."

☐ "You agreed to listen and hear me out. Stop interrupting or our conversation is over until you can remain calm."

☐ "It's not your place to scold me like a child. Please change your tone of voice and relate to me as an adult."

☐ "I'm not going to be made to feel guilty or ashamed about doing what I think is best for myself and my family—even if you disagree."

☐ "I'm sorry you're upset by my decision (my choice of churches, the way I discipline my children, or whatever), but you need to understand my right to live my life according to my own convictions."

☐ "I understand how you feel, but I'm not going to accept responsibility for your feelings. If you choose to be (upset, angry, depressed, and so on), then that is your choice—not my fault."

Realistically assessing your relationship with your father will help you predict which of the above responses might be needed to set a dialogue back on track. We strongly suggest that you memorize the statements you checked. Even if you don't trust yourself to say them out loud in a clam, nondefensive manner at first, you can still silently affirm them yourself. Many clients find it helpful to say these statements out loud to themselves when they begin to feel guilty, scapegoated, or out of control after a disturbing confrontation.

You will also want to limit the scope of your discussions. List the things you won't discuss with your father anymore (for example, your income or net worth, your weight or appearance, other members of the family):

- _____
- _____
- _____
- _____

You may choose to communicate your new ground rules on the phone, in a letter, or in person. Think about the most effective way that would work best for you. Even if the ground rules are clearly set, some of them involve things you cannot control without your father's cooperation. You will need to decide how you are going to respond if your father does not comply with the rules.

✔ Would you simply withdraw from the relationship for a specified time?

✔ Would you adjust your ground rules to reflect a reality you can live with?

✔ Would you let go of any hope of restored relationship and pray for a change of heart?

If the guidelines I set forth aren't respected, I will _____

_____

_____

_____ .

After you have met with your father, take time to reflect on the interaction:

When I told Dad about the new guidelines he _____

_____

_____ and I felt

_____

_____ .

What did I learn through this experience? _____

_____

_____

_____

What, if anything, will I do differently in the future? _____

_____

_____

_____

Saying Good-bye

If your father has died, has suffered poor health to the point of being unable to communicate, or is no longer part of your life, you may feel a deep need for a sense of closure in your relationship. It is often helpful to write a good-bye letter to your father and to your past, expressing all the emotion that is bottled up in your heart. You may need to write more than one letter to truly put the past behind you.

We encourage you to write the letter on a separate sheet of paper. Keep it in a safe place to refer to again in a few weeks when you are less emotionally involved. It is generally best not to show the letter to anyone and not to mail it to a disinterested father. You will be putting very private thoughts in print, and you may find it easiest to be totally honest if you decide before you ever begin that the letter will be destroyed promptly; that's fine. This exercise is between you and God for your own emotional well-being and personal growth.

Filling the Father Void

If your father did not, and still doesn't, meet your emotional needs, you will profit from godly role models. Chapter 6 ("Filling the Father Void") in *Father Memories* gives several constructive steps to take. For example, you can seek to build healthy friendships with older men of good reputation who can mentor you and pass along the type of fatherly advice and concern you missed out on. We suggest these guidelines for relating to a father-figure or mentor in a relationship:

1. *Look for someone who is a good role model and person of integrity.* Friends rub off on us in many ways. Values and beliefs are important, and in most cases theirs should be more solid and tested than ours.
2. *Look for someone who will be honest with you and who seeks accountability.* People who only tell you what you want to hear aren't real friends. It takes iron to sharpen iron—and sometimes that produces a few sparks.
3. *Look for someone who will set and maintain healthy boundaries with regard to how much help to give.* The goal in the relationship is to develop a healthy interdependence, not a dependent or codependent relationship. Avoid financial or emotional ties that control your behavior.
4. *For your closest friendships, choose someone of the same sex, even if you long for a father figure.* Every woman should be warned that many relationships with an older man that began innocently with a little fatherly advice developed eventually into immoral sexual involvement. Be sure healthy hedges are in place.

Do you think you would enjoy a close friendship with a man your father's age? Explain:

_____

_____

_____

_____

If you are feeling a father void and pray for a fatherly companion, yet things do not work out, it helps to remember that your Father in heaven is there for you at all times. He can, and is willing to, meet your needs, even when humans fail. In what ways has God helped fill your father void? _____

_____

_____

_____

_____

_____

Your Father as a Friend

When we reach adulthood, the parent/child relationship changes to and adult/adult interaction. This transition does nto always go smoothly, but it can be very rewarding. You may get to know your parents on another level and appreciate them more fully. As one man put it, "My silly old dad got smarter and smarter after I had kids of my own!"

Time spent together, shared interests, and common bonds help enhance any friendship. It is also important for friends to respect and appreciate one another, even their uniqueness and differences. Unfortunately, differences in personality, ability, or interests can cause friction. We need to learn to let me be me, and you be you, and still get along. And in some areas we may have to choose to disagree agreeably.

The following exercise will help you evaluate the similarities and differences between you and your father (or mother or child or friend). Rate yourself and your dad on each scale. If you and your father are talking and listening to each other, it may be fun to have your dad complete the same exercise without looking at your answers. Photocopy this page if you wish to share this exercise with your father, spouse, or other family members. You may be surprised to find that you don't always see each other the same way. And the conversation could lead to a few laughs and a deeper relationship.

Note: The scales are set up in random fashion and are not meant to imply any correlations between characteristics. Higher scores do not indicate superior or inferior ratings. There are no "right answers." The goal is simply improved understanding and open communication.

Appreciating Common Ground, Respecting the Differences

1	2	3	4	5	6	7	8	9	10
Security seeker									Risk taker

1	2	3	4	5	6	7	8	9	10
Feelings-oriented									Facts-oriented

1	2	3	4	5	6	7	8	9	10
Educated									Uneducated

1	2	3	4	5	6	7	8	9	10
Spontaneous									Planner

1	2	3	4	5	6	7	8	9	10
Outdoorsman									Indoorsman

1	2	3	4	5	6	7	8	9	10
Private									Public

1	2	3	4	5	6	7	8	9	10
Inadequate income									Surplus income

1	2	3	4	5	6	7	8	9	10
Night owl									Day lark

1	2	3	4	5	6	7	8	9	10
Quiet									Talkative

1	2	3	4	5	6	7	8	9	10
Republican									Democrat

1	2	3	4	5	6	7	8	9	10
Active & fast paced									Methodical & calm

1	2	3	4	5	6	7	8	9	10
Easy going & relaxed									Keyed up & intense

1	2	3	4	5	6	7	8	9	10
Time oriented									Not time oriented

1	2	3	4	5	6	7	8	9	10
Emotional									Stoic

1	2	3	4	5	6	7	8	9	10
Rigid									Flexible

Look back over your ratings. Which similarities have enhanced your relationship with Dad during childhood and now? _____

_____

_____

_____

How can you build on this common ground to improve your current relationship?

_____

_____

_____

Which differences of opinion or temperament have caused friction between you and your father through the years? _____

_____

_____

_____

What could you do to minimize these differences from now on? _____

_____

_____

_____

Do you see an imbalance in your life concerning any of these characteristics? _____

_____

_____

_____

Often these type of imbalances irritate others and make us harder to live with. List five ways you can begin to smooth off your rough edges and make your home life run smoother.

1. _____

2. _____

3. _____

4. _____

5. _____

Realistic Expectations: Letting Go of the Fantasy

Here is the formula for disappointment: Take your expectations, subtract reality, and the difference will equal your level of disappointment (Expectations − Reality = Disappointment Level).

How realistic were, or are, your expectations for your dad? _____

_____

_____

_____

Can you think of times you did, or do, expect more than he is capable of delivering?

_____

_____

_____

On the left-hand side of these blank lines, list the expectations you have, or had, for your father. List as many as possible. Be specific. For example, "I expected my father to respect my opinions," or, "I expected Dad to trust my judgment on night curfews." Then on the right-hand side list the reality for each of the expectations—perhaps "When Dad was tired he was a poor listener and his opinion always won out," or, "Dad just told me when to get home without trusting me."

My expectation was or is . . .   The reality was or is . . .

_____   _____

_____   _____

_____   _____

_____   _____

_____   _____

_____   _____

_____   _____

_____   _____

_____   _____

_____   _____

_____   _____

_____   _____

_____   _____

Based on the disppointment formula above, look over your expectations and realities and write a specific list of disappointments that stem from the difference between your expectations and reality. I am disappointed that

- _____
- _____
- _____
- _____
- _____

     If you can lower your expectations to line up with reality, you will experience less disappointment and friction in your relationship. Sometimes you must simply grow up and go on. This exercise is not designed to excuse your father's present or past behavior. It is simply a way for you to face reality as it is and in the process improve your relationship.

Based on what I know, or knew, or my father's temperament and capacity to love me as his son or daughter, I expect my father to _____

_____

_____

_____

_____

_____

_____

Disappointment is a two-way street. Can you think of ways in which your father's expectations for you have not fit the reality of who you are or how you want to respond?

_____

_____

_____

How has this mismatch of expectations made your father feel let down in the past?

_____

_____

_____

_____

Often these expectations are unspoken or implied rather than expressed directly. We strongly encourage you to talk openly with your father about what you needed from him as a child—and want from him now as an adult. Also talk over what he needed from you as a child and wants from you now as an adult. If at all possible, these conversations are best conducted one-on-one in a private place.

Do you think you could improve your relationship with your father by getting these things out in the open? _____

_____

What, if anything, would make you nervous about initiating this type of conversation?

_____

_____

Often we have inflated fears about discussing personal things. What is the worst thing that could happen? _____

_____

How would you handle it? _____

_____

What is the best outcome you can envision? _____

_____

How would you respond? _____

_____

Is it time you had a heart-to-heart talk with your father? Take the first step today.

The journey of ten thousand miles begins with a single phone call.
Confucius Bell

Honoring Your Father

There are eight specific times in Scripture where we are told to honor our fathers, and additional references instruct us to honor our parents. There is a promise connected with the Fifth Commandment: "Honor your father and your mother, as the Lord your God has commanded you, so that you may live long and that it may go well with you in the land the Lord your God is giving you."[1]

Honoring your father in the biblical sense has to do with living a wise and clean life that does not bring shame to the family name, for "sin is a disgrace to any people."[2]

After reading each verse listed below, fill in a few of your own thoughts about what it means to honor your parents:

1. "A wise son brings joy to his father, but a foolish man despises his mother."[3]

_____

_____

2. "To have a fool for a son brings grief; there is no joy for the father of a fool."[4]

_____

_____

3. "For God said, 'Honor your father and mother'; and 'Anyone who curses his father or mother must be put to death.' "[5]

_____

_____

4. "The eye that mocks a father, that scorns obedience to a mother, will be [punished.]."[6]

_____

_____

5. "He who robs his father and drives out his mother is a son who brings shame and disgrace."[7]

_____

_____

6. "Listen to your father, who gave you life, and do not despise your mother when she is old."[8]

_____

_____

To honor your father means to show respect, regardless of whether you never or seldom received respect from him. God didn't intend for us to take this command as a suggestion. Little children were to be obedient and respectful, never mouthy or lazy. And adult children were to take care of aging parents and speak respectfully. Adults, however, were required to obey God and _listen_ to their father—not necessarily _obey_ all that he said.

The concept of honor revolves around an attitude of investing someone with worth, holding someone in esteem because of their God-given value and position as your parent. The concept of honor does not imply that you must like your father's character or choices, obey him no matter what, or spend lots of time together. Honor simply means that you respect your father in word and behavior, treating him with the dignity you hope others will extend to you.

Is honoring your father a problem for you? Explain. _____

_____

_____

_____

When was the last time you honored your father in word or behavior? _____

_____

_____

What did you do? _____

_____

Here are several ways you can honor your father. Check those you have done or are willing to try. If your father is deceased, check those things your dad did while he was alive.

- ☐ Write your dad a letter and let him know you are praying for him.
- ☐ Reach out to keep communication open after disagreement.
- ☐ Find a gift that your father would like and send it to him for no reason other than your appreciation of him.
- ☐ Tell one person something positive about your father.
- ☐ Speak well of your parents in front of your children.
- ☐ Write or call a sibling to discuss a positive father memory you have in common.
- ☐ Tell your father "thank you" for all that he has invested in your life.
- ☐ Refuse to take part in any "put-down sessions" behind your father's back.
- ☐ Shift your attitude away from superiority, rebellion, contempt, or disrespect.
- ☐ Call your father by name, rather than "*he* said that" or "*he* wants us to come"; say, "Dad said that," or, to your children, "Grandpa wants us to come."
- ☐ Think of three positive stories to tell your children about their grandfather.

What specific things are you willing to do this week to demonstrate honor and respect for your father? Begin with the attitude of your heart, then with the words of your mouth, and then outward actions.

_____

_____

_____

Resolution and Moving On

Enjoying Your Relationship with Your Heavenly Father

We were created in the image of God and can enjoy the privilege of being His children. Here are a few things God promises to do for His children. Consider each promise and its effect on your life.

God gives us Life:

"O Lord, you are our Father. We are the clay, you are the potter; we are all the work of your hand."[1]

God has compassion on us:

"As a father has compassion on his children, so the Lord has compassion on those who fear him."[2]

God disciplines us:

"The Lord disciplines those he loves, as a father the son he delights in."[3]

God gives good gifts:

"If you, then, though you are evil, know how to give good gifts to your children, how much more will your Father in heaven give good gifts to those who ask him!"[4]

God is merciful:

"Be merciful, just as your Father is merciful."[5]

God works in our behalf:

Jesus said, "My Father is always at his work to this very day, and I, too, am working."[6]

God welcomes any person who believes in Christ to be His child:

"I will be a Father to you, and you will be my sons and daughters, says the Lord Almighty."[7]

In what ways have the exercises in this journal helped you to realize and appreciate your position in Christ as a child of God? _____

_____

_____

_____

Do you feel like you know and enjoy your Father in heaven better now? ☐ Yes ☐ No

Explain your answer: _____

_____

_____

_____

_____

An Evening to Remember

Plan an evening to get together with your parents. During dinner or an enjoyable activity, have your parents share their childhood memories. Ask questions about your dad's father memories. See if you can gain insight into the man he is today. Share your own father memories and talk about what you wanted and received from him. If you feel comfortable doing so, tell him what you have been learning about yourself. Avoid criticizing or becoming upset; instead focus on using the conversation to open communication and draw you closer to each other.

Creating New Memories

When you picture yourself as a parent there are probably some ways in which you want the script of your children's childhood memories to be different from your own. If you have children, set about to create for them the happy memories that meant the most to you. Then go back to the painful memories you listed and rewrite them the way you want them to be if a similar situation comes up when you are the parent. Deliberately envision ways to break out of the negative cycle and take constructive steps to improve your relationship with your own children. As an adult, you are now in a position of power to create a new history from here on out!

Reaching Your Goals

Earlier in the journal, on page 23, we asked you to list the things you hoped to accomplish by working through these exercises. Take time now to evaluate your efforts. Do you feel you reached your goals? Explain your answer:

_____

_____

_____

List the five most powerful insights you gained or the principles that you feel will have the greatest impact on your life:

1. _____

2. _____

3. _____

4. _____

5. _____

What is the most important lesson you want to take away from this experience? _____

_____
_____
_____
_____

_____

You have worked hard completing this journal. It's time to reward yourself for a job well done!

Notes

How to Use This Workbook

1. Malachi 4:6.
2. Genesis 1:27.
3. Ephesians 1:5, TLB.
4. John 1:11-12, TLB.
5. Psalm 68:5-6, NASB.

PART ONE: YOUR FATHER MEMORIES

What Do You Recall?

1. American Psychiatric Association, *Diagnostic and Statistical Manual of Mental Disorders*, 3d ed., rev. (Washington, D.C., 1987).
2. Quoted in Randy Carlson, *Father Memories: How to discover the unique, powerful, and lasting impact your father has on your adult life and relationships* (Chicago: Moody, 1992), 30.
3. Daniel Gottlieb and Edward Claflin, *Family Matters: Healing in the Heart of the Family* (New York: NAL/Dutton, 1991), 9.

Understanding the Foundation Your Father Set

1. 1 Peter 5:7.
2. 1 John 4:19.
3. Isaiah 66:13; Deuteronomy 1:31.

PART TWO: MAKING THE MOST OF YOUR MEMORIES

Your Personal Perception

1. Kevin Leman and Randy Carlson, *Unlocking the Secrets of Your Childhood Memories* (Nashville: Nelson, 1989), 14.

Drawing Strength from the Past

1. R. C . Sproul, *In Search of Dignity* (Ventura, Calif.: Regal, 1983), 28.
2. Ibid., 28-29.
3. Ibid., 29.

Men, Women, and Memories

1. Steve Farrar, *Point Man: How a Man Can Lead a Family* (Portland: Multnomah, 1990), 41.
2. Proverbs 9:8; 17:10.
3. Proverbs 17:27.
4. Proverbs 23:4-5.
5. Proverbs 23:20-21.
6. Proverbs 27:23-24.
7. Genesis 2:24.
8. Proverbs 23:20-21.

Authority Figures and Safe Leadership

1. 1 John 1:9.
2. M. Scott Peck, *The Road Less Traveled* (New York: Simon & Schuster, 1978), 24 (italics added).

PART THREE: TRUTH TO SET YOU FREE

Seeing God in the Image of Your Dad

1. Robert Hemfelt, Frank Minirth, and Paul Meier, *We Are Driven: The Compulsive Behaviors America Applauds* (Nashville: Nelson, 1991), 190-91, as quoted in Randy Carlson, *Father Memories: How to discover the unique, powerful, and lasting impact your father has on your adult life and relationships* (Chicago: Moody, 1992), 91-93.

2. Romans 8:15-17.
3. John 3:16.
4. 2 Peter 3:9.
5. Malachi 3:6.
6. Romans 2:6.
7. Ephesians 2:4.
8. Micah 7:18.
9. Lamentations 3:22-23.
10. Leviticus 11:44, NASB.
11. Psalm 25:8.
12. Nahum 1:7.
13. Numbers 23:19.
14. Hebrews 6:18.
15. John 14:6.
16. 2 Timothy 3:17, NASB.

Taking Responsibility for Yourself

1. M. Scott Peck, *The Road Less Traveled* (New York: Simon & Schuster, 1978), 35.
2. Malcolm X, *Malcolm X Speaks* (New York: Merit, 1965), 9.
3. Hebrews 11:6.
4. Richard Fowler and Rita Schweitz, *Together on a Tightrope: How to Maintain Balance in Your Relationships When Life Has You Off Balance* (Nashville: Nelson, 1992), 26. Used by permission.

You Have Choices; You Can Change

1. 2 Timothy 1:7.

PART FOUR: DEALING WITH YOURSELF, YOUR FATHER, AND OTHERS NOW

Stepping Ahead in Life

1. Sidney Simon and Suzanne Simon, *Forgiveness: How to Make Peace with Your Past and Get on with Your Life* (New York: Warner, 1990, 80.
2. Ibid., 96.
3. 1 Peter 5:6-7, NASB.
4. Simon and Simon, *Forgiveness,* 120.
5. Shad Helmstetter, *Choices* (New York: Pocket Books, 1989), 34.

Your Father As a Friend

1. Deuteronomy 5:16.
2. Proverbs 14:34.
3. Proverbs 15:20.
4. Proverbs 17:21.
5. Matthew 15:4.
6. Proverbs 30:17.
7. Proverbs 19:26.
8. Proverbs 23:22.

Resolution and Moving On

1. Isaiah 64:8.
2. Psalm 103:13.
3. Proverbs 3:12.
4. Matthew 7:11.
5. Luke 6:36.
6. John 5:17.
7. 2 Corinthians 6:18.

Seminars and conferences by Randy L. Carlson
on the following topics are available:
Father Memories; Early Childhood Memories; Marriage; Parenting

You may contact Mr. Carlson by writing or calling:
Today's Family Life
Box 37,000
Tucson, Arizona 85740
602-742-6976

Moody Press, a ministry of Moody Bible Institute,
is designed for education, evangelization, and edification.
If we may assist you in knowing more about Christ
and the Christian life, please write us without obligation:
Moody Pres, c/o MLM, Chicago, Illinois 60610.